Journey into More

Torn Curtain Publishing
Wellington, New Zealand
www.torncurtainpublishing.com

© Copyright 2020 Stephanie Herbert. All rights reserved.

ISBN Softcover 978-0-6489823-0-2
ISBN EPUB 978-0-6489823-3-3

No portion of this book may be reproduced, stored in a retrieval system or transmitted in any form or by any means—electronic, mechanical, photocopy, recording or otherwise—except for brief quotations in printed reviews of promotion, without prior written permission from the author.

Scripture quotations marked (NIV) are taken from the Holy Bible, New International Version®, NIV®. Copyright © 2011 by Biblica, Inc.™ Used by permission of Zondervan. All rights reserved worldwide. www.zondervan.comThe "NIV" and "New International Version" are trademarks registered in the United States Patent and Trademark Office by Biblica, Inc.™ Scripture quotations marked (AMP) are taken from the Amplified Bible, Copyright © 2015 by The Lockman Foundation. Used by permission. Scripture quotations marked (ESV) are from the ESV® Bible (The Holy Bible, English Standard Version®), copyright © 2001 by Crossway, a publishing ministry of Good News Publishers. Used by permission. All rights reserved. Scripture quotations taken from the (NASB®) New American Standard Bible®, Copyright © 1995, 2020 by The Lockman Foundation. Used by permission. All rights reserved. www.lockman.org. Scripture quotations marked (TPT) are from The Psalms: Poetry on Fire, The Passion Translation©, copyright © 2014. Used by permission of BroadStreet Publishing Group, LLC, Racine, Wisconsin, USA. All rights reserved. Scripture quotations marked (MSG) are taken from THE MESSAGE. Copyright © 2002. Used by permission of NavPress Publishing Group. Scripture quotations marked NLT are taken from the Holy Bible New Living Translation, copyright 2015 by Tyndale House Foundation. Used by permission of Tyndale House Publishers, Inc., Carol Stream, Illinois 60188. All rights reserved.

Cover art by Elesa Stellios ©2020

Cataloguing in Publishing Data
Title: Journey into More
Author: Stephanie Herbert
Subjects: Personal memoir, Christian life, Spirituality

Journey into More

STEPHANIE HERBERT

Thanks be to God, I was brought up in a loving family with a strong Christian heritage and I grew up in a church that loved and taught the Word of God.

Thanks be to God, after marrying an amazing man also brought up in a loving Christian home, I went through a spiritual wilderness. During that time, I continued to attend church and Bible studies. I volunteered and did all the other things 'nice' Christians do.
But it wasn't enough. It was never meant to be.

This is the story of how God walked me out of my wilderness, into more of Him.

May this journey continue till the day I am truly Home.

Contents

1. The Wilderness 9
2. Just One Step 13
3. Worship 17
4. Heritage 20
5. His Word 24
6. A Word 28
7. Overcomer 32
8. Barriers 37
9. Journaling 41
10. Dreams 45
11. Worship Wider 51
12. Just One Word 54
13. Fear 57
14. Mindsets 62
15. Vision 68
16. One Cedar 72
17. Worship Deeper 76
18. Order 82
19. Balance 86
20. Forest of Cedars 90

21.	Little Foxes	94
22.	Obedience	98
23.	Worship Higher	103
24.	Adore. Abide	105

1
The Wilderness

I am worn out from my groaning.
All night long I flood my bed with weeping
and drench my couch with tears.
My eyes grow weak with sorrow;
they fail because of all my foes.
Psalm 6:6-7 NIV

Where do you start with a journey that has been going on for so long?

Approaching my fiftieth year seemed like an appropriate time to contemplate where my life was heading. Most of the women around me who were already into their fifties seemed to be settled in their careers. As a home educating mother, however, it seemed a bit late for me to start one!

As I looked around, I saw women who had given much of their lives to raising children. Now their children were grown, those women had more 'freedom' in their lives to do other things—

and yet I noticed that often those other things did not seem to be centred around their homes, their families, or their faith. As a home educator my heart grieved. Where were the spiritually mature women? Who would mentor the young mums? Why were so few of us developing a closer relationship with our husbands as we approached the retirement years? Where were the wise women of faith, the ones who always had a good shoulder to lean on? They had always been around when I was growing up, whether I truly valued them or not. But where were they in my generation?

And anyway, where was I? I had been in a spiritual wilderness for quite a few years. In fact, I spent most of my forties in a place of loneliness, pain, fear . . . great fear, and frustration, simply going through the motions as a wife, mother, home educator, woman, daughter, friend, and volunteer.

Soon after turning forty, we had moved from a quiet rural town to a regional city. I had two panic attacks around the time of the move but never thought much of it. The first year in our new home I caught a cold which resulted in tinnitus, or continuous loud ringing in one ear, for the next two years. This affected all my relationships; my whole-body stress levels skyrocketed during that time. Concurrently, the pain in my gut meant my diet became increasingly restricted.

When I looked at the few areas in my life where I was putting in all my effort, it seemed that despite giving it my best, failure was certain. I had always feared failure—I didn't need a psychologist to tell me that. And then there were the feelings of rejection and unworthiness that I had carried for many years. Anxiety grew unabated.

Some dietary changes helped improve my anxiety levels and my gut symptoms. But only just. There were still many times when I would be going somewhere and then turn the car around and head back home to check I hadn't left the stove on. Other times I fought the urge, but only just. I had even developed strategies and patterns to make sure I checked the stove. I told myself good things, the old 'positive talk.' But despite all my efforts, I couldn't hide the fear. Maybe I could hide it from others, but not from myself. It surrounded me and travelled with me through every step of life.

And my faith? Where was *it*? Well, that was a good question! It felt kind of ... *dead*! It was there, though. I was helping at church. I was singing. I was serving. I was going to home group. I seemed to know all the right Bible answers, yet I rarely actually picked up my Bible. Quite frankly, after more than forty years, I found it boring. I'd read it all before. Or so I told myself, although I'd never actually read the whole thing. I prayed, but it was always 'on the go.' I wasn't good at routine anyway. That made for a good excuse. I was just coasting along, being a 'nice' Christian because, of course, growing up in the eighties in Canada, the imperative seemed to be: *be nice, try hard*. So I just tried to keep it up.

Somewhere along the line I had heard the general idea of the Christian life was to, 'Adore God. Abide in God.' I had even written it on a little scrap of paper and stuck it on my dresser mirror. I thought I was doing it. I certainly did the right actions, didn't I? Yet I knew I was not living my idea of 'the victorious Christian life,' and as I thought about turning fifty, I knew either this must not be our purpose as Christians, or I simply wasn't doing it well enough. It still sounded like a nice idea in principle—it left me with the fact that I wasn't measuring up. I was trying the best I knew how, but that only fed the guilt.

I couldn't shake this nagging feeling that there should be... more.

That I should be praying... more.

Adore God.

Abide in God.

Wasn't I?

2
Just One Step

He lifted me out of the pit of despair, out of the
mud and the mire. He set my feet on solid
ground and steadied me as I walked along.
Psalm 40:2 NLT

All it took initially was one step. It only ever takes one step to change your direction, though often we don't realise the magnitude of that step until much later.

As I chatted with a friend recently, I realised there was a distinct turning point in my walk. It came well before I was aware of actively seeking for more. It came while the cloud of darkness and discouragement was still very heavy over me.

It was a weekday afternoon. Not too hot, not too cold . . . just right.

Just right for the Lord to work.

Just right, because I was a mess.

I was sitting on the floor of my bedroom, leaning against the end of my bed, balling my eyes out. I had yelled at my son yet again. Yet again I had hurt my tender-hearted boy. Even so, he held out his arms to give me a cuddle, perhaps because he could see I was hurting too. I had ranted and raged at him about something, probably about some way that he, my sensitive son with learning delays and complex medical issues, wasn't meeting my perfectionist adult expectations.

I lived so many of those days with extremely high stress levels in my body. The constant buzzing in my ears which reverberated throughout most of my head seemed to cause the rage to simmer on the inside of me, barely with a lid on, and it all too regularly boiled over. I hated it. Every time it spilled out, I hated it. Every time I vowed 'never again.' Every time, I tried to apologise to my son, even if it took me a while. And for his part, he forgave me and told me he loved me . . . every time.

As I sat on the floor, my eyes staring out of my empty self, I absently scanned the bookshelf and noticed my Bible. It was on my bookshelf because I was not reading it! I hadn't for quite a while. The days of trying hard were already long enough. But as I looked at it that day, I longed to pick it up once again. I knew it would make me feel better, even just to hold it. There had been other days when I had held the Bible in my hands, and it just felt so good, so comforting. But that day I was lower than ever, so low I feared to pick it up. I knew it would make me feel better, yet as I thought about opening it, I felt scared.

I knew something was wrong with my response; it was not good. And yet I felt incapable of moving, either physically or emotionally, away from all the pain and fear. So I stared longingly at my Bible on the shelf, as if staring at it would somehow draw the comfort out of my Bible and into me.

And then inside of me, out of a deep black hole, I began yelling out uncontrollably to God. *'You said . . . You said . . . You said it's not supposed to be like this! I don't want to live in this wilderness. It sucks! Please take me out of here, God, please! I have no idea what to do. I don't know how to get out of here.'* I was angry at Satan too, and I turned and yelled at him as well. *'No more! This is enough! Get out of here! Leave me alone!'*

God hears all our prayers, but He especially loves the deeply heartfelt ones—the ones we pray when we are at the end of our rope. When we finally realise we can't do it ourselves. When we give up trying. And that's where I was at.

I didn't see the answer straight away, however. Initially I don't think I was even aware of any physical change. But looking back, I can see He was at work. Finally, I had given up on 'me' solving it all. I had admitted I could not do it anymore and I needed Him. My admission was the precursor to an answered prayer! I have since found that for me the fastest way to start moving towards an observable, physical breakthrough is by surrendering the situation to God.

Of course, that doesn't mean God hasn't already been working. To surrender a situation to Him consciously and willingly requires us to lay it down spiritually, in our hearts. In that place, I have no doubt He has been deeply at work much longer than we realise. So deeply at work, in fact, we usually can't see it. And all the while, He's been softening our hearts to His voice. Preparing us.

Finally, I had gotten to the point where I hated what Satan was doing in my life more than I liked the idea of solving it myself. We may say we are willing to submit a situation to God, but often it's not as easy as it sounds, at least not to start with. It gets easier once we admit there is no more rope left to hang on to and we realise our own brokenness. Ahh, *that* is the place where Jesus loves to work! His compassionate eyes pour out His love on us, as He stoops down to lift us up. Already He can see the beauty of the wholeness we are to walk into! Already, He declares what is not yet, as if it already is! Our beautiful Shepherd-King!

3
Worship

Lift your hands toward the sanctuary and praise the LORD.
Psalm 134:2 NLT

'You don't lift your hands in worship. That's a bit extreme, isn't it? Only emotional charismatics do that. Or maybe people who are really happy or thankful. Like, you would need a real reason to do that,' said the lie in my head.

The first sign of change in my life was lifting my hands during worship at church. I really enjoyed worship music, but until now, even when I had been seeking a closer relationship with the Lord, I don't remember raising my hands in worship. However, I do remember, when I first started to lift them, I didn't really feel like it yet! I remember feeling like I didn't really have anything to lift my hands about! But somehow it was like my body wanted to make a statement declaring there *was* something worth worshipping for, something more than what I had always sung about. I didn't yet know what the 'something more' was, but I was making a stand to believe there *must* be more, without seeing it yet. Oh yes! I was choosing faith! Faith to ignore the obvious I could see, and instead believe for better, to ignore everything I thought was wrong with my life, and just choose to sing about the goodness of God anyway. After all it was more enjoyable than looking at the mess of my life! *Thank you, Lord, for giving me a gift of faith in that moment, to step out towards You.*

But in that moment, two incredible things happened. First, I enjoyed praising God with my hands in the air! It felt *good!* It felt like I really *was* praising Him. Second, no one stared at me. No one looked at me as if I'd lost the plot. No one rejected me. That blew me away . . . and it gave me confidence.

Later, a visitor to our church who soon became a friend, helped me make sense of it. She said worship music 'changed spiritual atmospheres.' I had never consciously thought about worship music like that before, but now that she mentioned it, I knew it was true. It was like a heart-knowing I had forgotten about, and needed to be reminded of. So I started to play the few worship albums I had at home and listen to Christian radio in the car. I knew the atmosphere needed to be changed.

Then God showed me a slightly bigger picture.

As I looked at my son in church one day, I saw a young boy who loved the Lord, but he never seemed to connect well with music. He didn't sing—he rarely did at all, even once he learned to read the words at the age of twelve. Often, he yawned. I instinctively knew what was going on—the music was overwhelming to his system. There was just way too much sensory input for him, especially when it was in live worship. I wondered . . . if I surrounded him with more music, would he just get used to it?!

Observing my son inspired me to play music even more often, over and over. And not only did playing the music start to impact my son, but our relationship became richer again as we enjoyed the music together. Soon, the music was sinking deeper into my heart, then it started to come *from* my heart. The Lord was waking up my heart using the music I had always loved, but He was taking it to a deeper level. Indeed, the atmosphere was shifting! My heart was shifting. My spirit was waking up. I still carried lots of fear. But I was starting to carry a bit more of Jesus too.

4

Heritage

Train up a child in the way he should go;
even when he is old he will not depart from it.
Proverbs 22: 6 ESV

Growing up in a Christian environment, I came to believe that, as Christians, we simply accept Jesus as our Saviour and all our sins are forgiven. Period. Don't get me wrong—all our sins *are* forgiven; it's pretty awesome. But it seemed as though that was the limit of what had fully established in my heart.

How had my internalised understanding of this thing called 'Christian faith' become so small? Was I taught bad theology? Or did I just not understand what I was taught? Had I preferentially forgotten the other bits of it? Surely, all those years of summer camp, Bible study, church and youth group didn't come down to just that?! Or perhaps it had something to do with the intervening adult years when I had become more interested in myself than God?

No matter how it happened, somehow the entire message I believed always came back to something like: *You're forgiven, so be nice, do good, pray, try hard . . . and then, one day, you'll go to heaven.* Somewhere along the line I had accepted that I should either improve myself, my character and habits, by striving—or, wait for my perfection, which would finally come when I got to heaven.

On reflection, at least two things were absent in my internalised understanding, the first being the idea of intimate, two-way communication with the Lord. As a child I had grasped the concept of a personal relationship with Jesus—in fact, I'm sure it was the only way I made it through a lonely childhood of being ostracised. I remember chatting away to Him a lot in my lonely times and my times of being bullied. I took great comfort from knowing Jesus had been bullied and ostracised too.

My young years held much sound advice about prayer. But while I often chatted to Jesus, I don't remember anyone really telling me how to hear Him talk to *me*. Or that He should. I just presumed He spoke through the Bible—which, of course, He does! But I didn't have any expectation of hearing Him speak to me personally, individually. There were times during my adult life when I had felt closer to God, and at those times I think I was more aware of Him prompting me. But those times always seem to have been cut off. Invariably, something would come up and would throw me off course, leaving me discouraged.

Perhaps I thought only people who were going into ministry or coming out of some terribly sad lifestyle, heard God 'talk' to them. Somehow it just didn't seem like it happened to everyday people with everyday issues. That's what the Bible was for, I presumed. I had a brain and believed I was expected to use it. If I looked at my life, I could see what I liked and was good at, and I just went forward from there. My decisions were primarily based on logic and rational thoughts.

The second thing absent in my faith was an understanding of spiritual freedom and authority. I think somehow my theology ended up being that once I gave my life to Christ, I was just supposed to 'cope' with whatever came my way. Yes, cope with the strength God gave me, but basically, put up with whatever came my way. Life was about coping with what you got dished out, and *overcoming* was some sort of code for 'still going to church when you die.'

Why did I never realise or internalise the idea that I could be free of pains such as shame and rejection that kept me from being more of who I wanted to be? I knew I would be free of them in eternity, but that seemed a long way away. Did I hear about the truth of spiritual freedom but then forget it as the stresses of life clamoured back in? Or perhaps it all seemed like too much hard work? Whatever the reason, I was left carrying emotional and physical burdens I knew Christ had died for, which only left me with another burden: guilt.

As a young person I was, however, taught lots about how to grow in my faith through Bible reading, prayer, study, attending services . . . you know, the usual habits and disciplines. In and of themselves they are all good, but on their *own*, without the Holy Spirit's involvement, they are just religion. My faith was often limited to the form, the habit, the 'doing', and all the while the 'being in a relationship' aspect of my faith was significantly dampened as life got busier and other things came along, until the relationship was nearly squashed. The Word of God became dead words on a page. The Christian habits that continued in my life became religion. Some people might be good at religion. I've realised I'm not. Which probably explains why my faith was dead—or at least deeply asleep—for those years. It exposed the weaknesses in my walk. The habits I managed to keep up helped me stay afloat . . . but only barely.

And yet, the Holy Spirit moved. I look back at my teen years and I can see Him moving—at youth meetings, at summer camp. I had some truly beautiful, serene times; I just didn't know it was the Holy Spirit among us! No one said so. I didn't know how to enable it, or how to experience it more. I didn't know there *was* more, or that there was even meant to be more! But I think somehow those special Holy Spirit moments laid a seed. Oh, how the Lord waits patiently for us to seek Him, and keep on seeking Him, with all our heart! Sometimes seeds take a long time to hatch.

Now, all these years later, He was moving again. In all reality, He never stopped moving—I just stopped being aware of it for many years. I had stopped listening or being willing to respond. That's why the end of the rope was such an effective place to be! Like a rejected suitor that will not quit, He was there to woo me again. I had invited Him into my place of pain.

5

His Word

---

*Break open your word within me until
revelation-light shines out! Those with open
hearts are given insight into your plans. I open
my mouth and inhale the word of God because I
crave the revelation of your commands.*
Psalm 119:130-131 TPT

Gradually, ever so gently, Holy Spirit led me back to His Word. He led me to look at different versions, so I had variety instead of just the one I had been reading for years. And gradually the hunger for His Word grew again.

Then He led me to a new study group—as these friends delved into deeper questions with me, the Bible seemed to become more personal. The questions we explored were different to the boring ones I had heard so often before! Gently, gently, lest I should fear I was being too extreme or turning into one of those 'Jesus nerds,' He called me closer. He showed me His Word and I craved it. I studied it. Even this seemed kind of weird and extreme, but also rather . . . nice! Quite lovely, really! The new versions of Scripture really helped, especially *The Passion Translation*. A friend had given me a copy of the Psalms and Proverbs in that version for my fiftieth birthday. Oh, what beautiful expression of the Psalms! And oh, how I still love the Psalms!

About eight months later, I came across a free online resource produced by Anne Graham-Lotz which I really enjoyed. She gave a brief introduction about how to study the Bible; it was quite an intuitive approach and could be used for any passage of Scripture. Now, as I read my Bible, I got so much more out of it! Suddenly, it was relevant and applicable to me—it was like a personalised study! After trying the method on a few passages of Scripture, I wondered what to study next. I spent some time looking at the contents page of my Bible. I knew I wanted to study something in the New Testament, so I read through the names of the books, asking God to show me what to read. One seemed to jump off the page . . . it was the book of Hebrews. Yes, the *whole book*! It seemed daunting, so I decided I'd just do part of it and see how it went.

I began studying, four verses at a time. What joy! I didn't get to it every day, and it took me longer than I wanted, but oh, how I enjoyed it! Some days I found myself writing pages of thoughts as I pondered just one verse. I was hooked! Even now, when someone mentions a verse from the book of Hebrews, my heart lifts as they say it. I might not remember the exact verse, but my love for the book has grown so much. It's as if it is *mine* now, as if I have some sort of ownership of it! It's personal.

I was surprised at the next book the Lord led me to—Isaiah. And yes, I'm still going on it! It contains so many awesome promises, such beautiful pictures of the future! For a lover of Handel's *Messiah,* it is so nice to study those verses in context. The book of Isaiah is full of treasures! I don't study it four verses at a time as I did Hebrews, but still it elevates my heart and my soul every time I sit with it. I relish the words, their meanings, their insinuations and implications, and the beautiful pictures they paint. Healing. Faithfulness. Redemption. Restoration. Visions of the Throne Room. Did I say Scripture has come alive to me?!

Now I absolutely love my Bible. I love it when I sit with my Bible as Holy Spirit preaches beautiful sermons with great love, great relevance, to me. When I open my Bible, it is like I open up my own personalised treasure chest; anticipation rises as I look inside with expectant awe for what my perfect Counsellor will show me that day.

The Jewish scholars typically say there are four levels of understanding Scripture: literal, implied, metaphorical/allegorical, and the hidden meaning. So, in addition to fully understanding the English words used in Scripture and the implications for our lives, there is still so much the Lord can show us. Sixty-six books at four levels of understanding, plus my own understanding as I grow in Him? I think I have enough to keep me going for many years yet!

Still, the realities of life intrude into my quiet times. These are good things, necessary activities, therefore it takes ongoing effort to protect my time with the Lord. Some days, even though

I crave it, the activities of life keep me from study. But I do not dwell on this, because I find it is an easy way for guilt and legalism to get a hold. The difference now is that my relationship is not with a book, but with the God of the universe. Our relationship doesn't stop when I put down my Bible! And I do not read because I must or I should, but because it brings me delight. Oh, the rest that is available there! Time spent engaging with my heavenly tutor in His Word is the best stress-buster I know! It draws the world out of me; it draws me aside from the world to encounter His immeasurable love afresh. Funnily enough, when my time with Him in the Word comes to a close, I find it enriches my engagement, not only with my Lord, but with the world as well!

6
A Word

---

*When someone prophesies, he speaks to
encourage people, to build them up,
and to bring them comfort.*
1 Corinthians 14:3 TPT

Some time later, a friend came to me with 'a word!' I'd heard of the concept, but I'd never received a 'prophetic word' for myself. The church congregations I had been involved with didn't prophecy, so I had never been exposed to it. I had been given verses before, and some of them 'rang true' for me, but in those cases, I surmised that whoever gave it to me just knew their Bible well. Clearly my assumption came from my own lack of understanding of how the Lord speaks!

This time, it was different. While my friend knew a bit about me, there was no way she could have known what was really going on in my life. Yet when I read what she had written, the words seared into my heart and spoke to me so deeply. She had a word for my son too. For days, every time I read it, I cried and cried.

It was beautiful and painful all at the same time, and it got me thinking. How did she do that? Oh, how I had underestimated God!

Soon after, my friend told me about a prophetic intercessor at her church and eventually my family and I arranged to meet with him, although I didn't know what to expect. None of us did really. But I was getting the idea there was much more of God to be had, and I was determined not to miss out any longer! Again, I cried and cried as the intercessor told me what the Lord wanted to say to me, through him. He too spoke of things no one else could possibly have known about. His words gently touched my heart in ways no person could ever do! It was *love* poured out, and it left me totally and completely undone.

My only response in both situations was to cry. But why was I crying? Surely a person knows what makes them cry! It is still hard to put into words, but what I know is that even now, my usual response to the manifest presence of Holy Spirit is to cry. Other people laugh when the Lord's presence draws near. Some just collapse. But I cry—a deep, gut-wrenching, sobbing cry. At least, that is how I have experienced Him so far. Several years later, it's still the same, yet it's never what I really expect—it just wells up in me and overtakes me. It flows out of some deep place.

Recently I asked Holy Spirit, 'Why do I cry?' and He replied, 'It's because of all those times you didn't cry.' Suddenly I recalled the many times in my childhood when I was in pain, when I felt rejection and so on, yet I just kept trying to hold it all together, trying to be strong. When the Holy Spirit spoke those words, I knew exactly what He meant, and once again, I was in tears . . . this time, tears of healing.

The tears I cried were tears of healing, but not just that, they were also tears of being known, of finally becoming aware I was truly, deeply known and yet still deeply loved. Tears of being loved from the very core of my being. Tears of desire—deep desire to walk into more of His presence. And even now, they are tears of surrender—sweet yet painful surrender, because in the moment I don't even know how to surrender myself to the extent I desire to. All I know is the tears flow as the dross is burned off, and even as I am aware of the depth of the surrender required, my heart calls out: *'More, Lord, more. I just need to know You more. I can't live without more of You.'*

As I experience more of the presence of the Lord, all I know is I need, I must have, still more. What is 'more'? After all, He gave all of Himself for me on the cross; He has given His all. Then why do I cry out for more? I think it is the deep heart desire to *know* Him more, to come further into alignment with Him and His ways. To continue to leave my sin-self nature behind and walk more deeply into the spirit-life and to experience all that was made available for me on the cross . . . all I was made for. To walk in my destiny.

As I cry before Him, healing takes place in the core of my being. As the needs in my spirit are met, it connects me more intimately with Holy Spirit, and something shifts on a level I cannot express in words. All I know is that He has healed depths of pain and brokenness I was not even truly aware of at the time. And yet in that very same instant, my desire, my deep need of Him, my awareness of my own un-holiness, is so heightened I feel totally lacking. I need more! My desire is to just draw closer to Him, to experience more of His love, His power, His presence and to do *whatever* and to lay down whatever I need to, that I may walk in continual communion with Him.

But back when my friend gave me that 'word,' I was not aware of any of that yet. I was just crying, and I didn't know why. I was way outside the comfort zone I had grown up in!

7

Overcomer

And they overcame and conquered him by the blood of the lamb and because of the word of their testimony.
Revelation 12:11 AMP

So, here I was, stepping out of my comfort zone. I knew what I had reduced my faith to over the years, and I knew where I was at, but I had no idea where I was going, or supposed to be going, on this journey. What did an abundant, Spirit-filled life look like? If my friend who prophesied over me and the intercessor from her church were good examples of Spirit-filled lives, then I would have to say it looked like God speaking personally to me in a way I could in some manner 'hear' and understand.

Hearing God speak personally to me sounded exciting! I had been learning to hear Him speak to me through His Word, so hearing with deeper insight and understanding sounded great! I knew it was possible. These people were not *that* much different than me.

As I considered what people had spoken over me, the word 'overcomer' stood out. And so, I looked up verses about overcoming. I read that to overcome Satan, which I was now aware I really wanted to do, I needed not only the blood of the Lamb, I also needed a testimony of what the blood of the Lamb had done for me. I started to read about what the blood does for me—until then, I had mostly just thought it cleansed me from my sins.

Apart from that, I didn't feel I had much to testify about what God or the blood was doing in my life, because I didn't feel I was seeing any sign of its effects. Testifying always seemed so huge anyway. I found it hard to speak about such personal things in public. And then I realised this wasn't necessarily talking about testifying in public! This was talking about testifying in the spirit, it seemed—in prayer.

It also included testifying *to myself*! I was being called to declare to myself and my situations, exactly what the blood does for me. To state it as true. In order to do that, I would have to know what the blood actually does for my situations, *and* believe it! I needed to learn to take the blood and make it personal and real in my life daily. This verse was calling me to *appropriate* the blood in every situation where the enemy attacked me. Wow! That sounded powerful! Now I was being called to stand up to my enemy with the blood of Jesus! That certainly sounded effective.

I knew from 2 Corinthians 5:17 I was a new creation in Christ; it's true, whether or not I believe it, see it, or even feel it. None of my observations or opinions actually affect its truthfulness! Just because it isn't obvious in my life yet does not change the reality—God's reality—of the situation. He sees me as a new creation; therefore, I can state it as truth. My job is to declare it as true, and then work with Holy Spirit to bring it about and make it manifest in my life. I've found that working with Holy Spirit mostly involves me yielding and Him moving!

From considering my readings in Hebrews again, I could see this book held much to help me understand more about the life and lifestyle of an Overcomer. Hebrews 3:12 in the Amplified version warns us not to have an 'unbelieving heart [which refuses to trust and rely on the Lord, a heart] that turns away from the living God.' I was starting to realise not only were there truths about God I did not fully believe with my mind; there were many more I did not believe deep in my heart. There were areas in my life where I was not trusting the Lord, areas where I was turning away from God and His teachings.

I would never have called myself a disbeliever, but not being patient and gentle with my son was one obvious place where I was not walking as God called me to. I had forgotten, or at least minimised the fact that I was a partaker of Christ; I was trying to trust in my own strength, and that approach was clearly failing. I was striving to be a perfectionist, when in Hebrews 7:11 perfection is described as 'a perfect fellowship between God and the worshiper'! My perfectionist tendencies were focused in the wrong direction. I was trying to ensure the world—and the people—around me were 'perfect' . . . and my personal view of perfect at that! But God's idea of perfection was altogether different!

I was like an Israelite who had not entered His rest (Heb 3:19). And yet, that rest was available to me! 'For we who . . .

personally trust and confidently rely on God . . . enter that rest so that we have His inner peace now because we are confident in our salvation, and assured of His power' (Heb 4:3 AMP). I didn't have inner peace—it was as simple as that! But oh boy, I was excited to know it was available to me! And, Hebrews 4:10 is clear about what rest actually looks like: 'For the one who has once entered His rest has also rested from [the weariness and pain of] his [human] labours, just as God rested from . . . His own.' I liked the sound of that! According to Hebrews 6, with confident hope that 'does not slip and cannot break down under whatever pressure bears upon it,' I am able to enter into the most Holy Place, to where the presence of God dwells, the place where Jesus is.

At the time, I didn't know what rest or being in God's presence was really like, but I was sure it was good, and the love I experienced when I received those prophetic words had sparked my desire for more of whatever there was to be had.

Perhaps not knowing His rest came ultimately back to me not really *knowing* God, not having a big enough picture of who He is. Hebrews 8:10 reminds me we are to both *know and experience* the love of God; Zechariah 8:8 speaks of both the mind *and* the heart. Experience is so much deeper than just head knowledge! It's true I have lots of 'head knowledge', but that's not the same as *experiencing* something!

What is it like to experience more of God? Hebrews 12:1-2 entreats us to strip off every weight and the sin which so easily entangles us, and to fix our eyes on Jesus. Jesus went to the cross so we may come to *maturity* in Him, not so we just 'get over the line' from death to eternal life.

God was calling me to an intimate relationship of full fellowship, communion and communication with Him. He was calling me to sanctify myself, so that I could be made mature in my faith (Heb 10:14) . . . a mature overcomer. He was calling me to leave my 'first covenant' of religious actions behind, to set myself apart to God and to be made mature by His hand rather than by my deeds. He was calling me to 'enter the Holy Place where He dwells' (Heb 10: 19-22), to come to Mount Zion and abide there (Heb 12:22). And not just when I die, but now, while I live!

At the time, I didn't understand much of what He was calling me to. Even now, I am aware there is much I don't fully understand. But the bit He had opened my eyes to sounded pretty awesome.

He was calling me closer.

He was calling me to *experience* Him.

I just needed to know where to start.

8

Barriers

---

*I have set before you life and death, the blessing
and the curse. So choose life in order that you
may live, you and your descendants.*
Deuteronomy 30:19 NASB

By now, one of my friends knew I wanted to get the bottom of this thing called 'knowing God,' and so, I was not surprised when she sent me a prayer regarding generational iniquity. Although this was a new concept to me, I could tell she had sent it in love, and that the Lord had prompted her. Never before had I really thought about the spiritual significance of what my ancestors had done, let alone whether or not they had sought repentance for their sins. It hadn't crossed my mind that their actions may have had any ongoing impact on me or affected me in any way.

My friend suggested I pray the prayer slowly, out loud, every night for seven nights, adding in repentance for anything the Lord brought to my mind as I did. I was amazed at just how much the Lord did bring to my mind! As I concentrated on the words of the prayer, random thoughts started 'popping' into my head—stories of my family I remembered hearing, and also impressions about things in my family history I had never heard spoken of. After all, no one really sings about all the iniquity in their family line! Each time I prayed the prayer, different words would 'leap off the page' at me or I would feel conviction in my heart about a certain aspect of the prayer. So, in a somewhat inexperienced but trusting manner, I simply asked the Lord for forgiveness and cleansing of those sins from my family line.

As I got towards the end of the week, I had a strong feeling I needed to pray this prayer for, and with, my dad. He lived overseas, and by then he had dementia and was not able to respond much on the phone. But I supposed his language processing was still there; and in any case, I felt it was important, so I organised to talk with Dad. As we spoke that night, and I explained to Dad what I wanted to do, I told him he could just pray the words in his heart if he agreed, and simply say 'Amen' at the end.

As I finished praying the prayer, he said 'Thank you.' It was very precious to hear him say those words. I don't know what spiritual difference it made to him or to our family line, but I will one day. It just felt like it needed to be done, and it was a significant and special time. The next time I saw Dad was when I spent a week visiting with him. During that time, I mostly read to him from Scripture. He would lie in bed, twiddling his thumbs on the waistband of his pyjamas, just as I remembered him doing when I was a child. He was happy and content. This was the last time I spent with him. Priceless.

When I look back at that prayer, I realise it was valuable in several ways. I believe it broke some things off my family lines, but it also opened my eyes to generational iniquity itself. Like everyone else, being the result of two complex family lines that extend all the way back to Adam, there was no shortage of issues to deal with! Yet I had rarely even thought about it . . . I think I just presumed it was all taken care of and covered when I accepted Christ—or perhaps when Jesus died. What I didn't realise until that moment was that I had to take hold of that blood and *utilise* it! I now had a new awareness of the need to personally appropriate the precious blood of Jesus.

Oh, how precious is the blood! It reminds me of the words of an old hymn about the blood of Jesus:

> *It makes me white as snow.*
> *No other font I know.*
> *Nothing but the blood of Jesus!*

Several years later I still, at times, find great value in praying 'set' prayers for personal and generational cleansing. These prayers (usually given to me by discerning friends or found online for specific purposes) have included prayers for deliverance from the effects of freemasonry. Often after these prayer times, I have experienced physical effects such as deep yawning, burping, or warm, tingling sensations in different parts of my body. These are in no way 'forced'—they are random responses within my body and their timing cannot be physically explained. These prayers, especially those against freemasonry, have also opened up to me deeper levels of vision and revelation than I have previously experienced.

Of course, we do not say these prayers 'by rote,' but with conviction and awareness (as much as possible) about what we are praying. The blood of Jesus is so, so powerful! It is all there—the healing is available! As we cry out and admit the rebellion of our forefathers, we can call on the blood of Jesus to cleanse us from any iniquity that we carry in our bloodlines. The enemy will use whatever he can to reduce or eliminate our effectiveness for the Kingdom here and now, but we have been given power in the name and by the blood of Jesus. Let's use it! As we do so, we enable the blessings the Lord has promised His people to be poured out on us; blessings that have been stolen by, or withheld from us, by the enemy! Jesus did not come to abolish the Law or the Prophets; instead, He came to fulfill them (Matthew 5:17). The enemy, however, still works within the Mosaic law; the results of iniquity are outlined there. The blood releases us from those effects if we 'put it on our doorposts,' applying it to our homes and families, just as God's people did during the Passover (Ex 12).

The Lord loves it when we are willing to step outside our comfort zone so His name may be magnified in our lives. You just never know what may await you on the other side!

9

Journaling

---

*My tongue is the pen of a ready writer. I speak
of things concerning my King.*
Psalm 45:1 NLT

Shortly after receiving prophetic prayer ministry and completing the initial generational iniquity prayers, I started to get dreams. Initially it was one a night, then more. I had no idea what the dreams meant. They seemed to make a bit of sense. But I didn't understand the symbolism of dreams. One dream seemed especially important, so I called my friend who was able to explain the symbolism for me. What she said made sense; it was appropriate to a situation I was facing at the time. But what also struck me was when she asked, 'You are writing all these things down, right?'

Oh dear! I admit I seriously flunk at doing a diary, or even using a planner. I have so many diaries that are wasted. Some of them are even really beautiful! I start the year intending to fill them up, but rarely do I make it beyond the beginning of March. So the idea of writing down what the Lord was showing me seemed overwhelming, to say the least. I would wake up in the morning with a vivid recollection of a dream and assure myself that, *of course I'd remember it!* Ha! Not likely! But I kept hearing that question in my head. I decided the next time I went to our local Christian bookshop I'd look for a nice journal. Maybe that would help!

Then one morning as I lay there thinking about the dream I had just had, I heard a distinct voice in my head loudly interrupting my thoughts and saying, 'So when are you going to start writing down what I say?!' Oh! I jumped out of bed, found an empty notebook on my bookshelf, and started writing what I remembered of the dream right then!

In fact, I wrote a lot—not just the details of the dream, but also what was on my heart and mind, other dreams and ideas, and the frustrations of life. As I gradually opened up to the process, I also started to write out my feelings. It was then I realised I had once written lots of long letters to my friends, especially as a young backpacker, but that was years ago. Now it was enjoyable to settle back into it. It was just like writing letters to God. It was beautiful . . . and settling, in an odd way. It seemed that as I wrote out my burdens, they became lighter.

Often, when I read over what I had written, I could see clearly where my ideas and impressions did not align with Scripture. That was a bit confronting! On other occasions I wrote good and godly ideas. Other times, fresh understanding popped into my mind as I wrote; I perceived these words were coming from Holy Spirit.

One day as I got to the end of what I had to write, I sensed there was more. It came as an impression in my heart, a soft answer. It was God's perspective, and it was loving and gentle. As I wrote down what seemed to be coming out of my heart, more words flowed. God was speaking to me in a way I had not previously experienced. It was beautiful and it blew me away because it was so personal, so gentle, so quiet, so . . . *healing*.

This form of communication has continued to grow and it is still incredibly special. Sometimes I simply lay out the questions that are on my heart and wait for His response. It always comes, and it's always beautiful, always gracious, always more full of love than I could imagine for myself. Sometimes it's even funny! Often it requires my action; it requires me to set aside time, pick up my journal, connect with God and write. The pen needs to be in my hand, *then* He speaks. Then other times, I simply hear, 'Not yet, just wait.' Sometimes when I have questions in my head through the day, He is quite clear—I need to journal to receive the answer. It certainly ensures I write the answer down!

I became more aware of the power of journaling and what it could be like when I read a book written by a friend of mine. In *'Feels Like I'm Breathing,'* Anya McKee walks her readers through a time when she was seeking the Lord for renewal in her own life, writing it all down in a two-way journal. It is a beautiful story, and so inspiring! It gave me the confidence that I wasn't just making it all up as I listened to the voice of God. As we step out into the unknown, it is lovely how the Lord brings people alongside us to encourage and confirm His work in our lives, especially when we start to walk into areas outside our norm, or outside where many of the people around us are heading. He is so awesome!

My journals filled up quickly—I have filled well over twenty now! Needless to say, I have moved from the nice, more expensive ones, to cheaper ones! There just seems to be so much to write out and pray to God. But then, it seems He has plenty to say to me too. At times I may not write for days, but I figure, there are no dates in a journal!

When I have been away too long, the Lord leads me back. He knows the responsibilities within my days and He also knows the needs of my heart. When I go back and look at what I have written I am amazed—I forget so much, and if I hadn't written it down, I would have had no record. Sometimes I am also amazed by how deep, personal and beautiful those journals are—I catch myself thinking, *'How did I ever write that?! They really aren't my words! They could only be the words of Holy Spirit. I don't write like that!* Like all letters between friends, I can see my relationship with the Lord changing and growing.

I love how You speak gently and quietly to me Lord. Thank you. You are so gracious and full of love. Open my ears so I may hear You better each day. Open my eyes so I may see You better, for in You there is light and love, freedom and security. Drawing aside with You fills me with peace and hope.

10

Dreams

When there is a prophet among you,
I, the LORD, reveal myself to them in visions,
I speak to them in dreams.
Numbers 12:6 NIV

I began journaling as a way of recording my dreams, but it had turned into so much more—a record of my conversations with God, as I learned to listen to His voice and share my thoughts and heart with Him too. As I got used to writing again, I realised journaling was, at least partially, about learning to steward the things of the Spirit that the Lord was giving me. It took time and effort. He was starting to call my priorities to change.

The dreams hadn't stopped, however, and I continued to write down my dreams as well. Sometimes I look back at dreams I have had previously, and the Lord brings me further understanding of what they mean. I should read them more, actually. I don't think I go back and read them enough. Every time I do, I learn so much about where I was in my walk, what the Lord was speaking to me about, and how my understanding of Him has changed.

The ways of our Father are so amazing. God never sleeps! And our spirit, the place where we are united with God's Holy Spirit, never sleeps. So it makes sense that God can—and would—minister and speak to us while we sleep! There are so many examples of this in the Bible—destiny dreams like those He gave to Jacob's son, Joseph, or warning and instructive dreams like the one He gave to Joseph, Jesus' earthly father.

For a long time, I believed dreams had no real value. I would, perhaps, have admitted to the worldly notion that your 'subconscious' gives you dreams. But despite all the examples in the Bible, I remained unwilling to believe God was speaking to me through dreams. As a result, I gave any dreams I had very little worth. Now I was realising I had not valued the move of the Spirit of God in my life. Oh, how much of the Lord I have missed out on over the years because of my lack of belief or willingness to be open to the ways He might move! Part of this came from my own ignorance of how He moves, or my lack of seeking Him for more, but as I came to Him in repentance for my stubbornness and ignorance, He comforted me, assuring me He knew the pain and the blockages I carried in my heart that had kept me from seeking more of Him. He knew how long it would take for me to come to Him humbly, in submission, and with a contrite heart. He knew my heart for Him, and He had walked me along that path to Him, even when I couldn't see it. Even when I was stubborn and stuck in my old ways.

As the Lord spoke to me through the night, I found He gave me different types of dreams, much like during Bible times.

At first, the dreams were really obvious, because my understanding was so limited, but He constantly encouraged me to seek for more insight and understanding, and soon my dreams became more complex, like a night-time parable! I had always appreciated the use of metaphor in literature; now my dreams carried some metaphor too!

I find God gives me dreams to help me know what is going on in my relationships with other people. By explaining them to me from a spiritual perspective, He gives me insight about how to pray into those relationships, or how I need to act. And sometimes He shows me where I have taken a wrong step. He brings conviction to me through my dreams! He has also given me spiritual understanding of situations where I was not involved, but had wondered what was going on.

Sometimes I receive dreams to warn me that I am coming to a time where I will need to choose to walk in Kingdom ways, not worldly ways. These dreams often involve me going down stairs. Recognising this has enabled me to be on alert and to be sure to live with my armour on! Dreams have also helped me understand where I have stumbled so that I can come before the Lord quickly in repentance to repair my relationship and intimacy with Him through appropriating that powerful blood!

As I sleep, God also gives me answers to questions I have asked Him during the daylight hours, when I was awake. Occasionally, He has even instructed me through dreams on how to make decisions that align with Kingdom principles and His desires. He has spoken to me about situations He wanted me to intercede for—situations I had no awareness of in the physical. The Lord has led me to intercede for international ministries I knew of, but had no contact with. He has also led me in how to intercede for someone in a court case. At one stage He warned me of an impending terrorist attack; it was exactly this dream that prompted me to find a group of intercessors where I could be supported to discern and pray into the dreams I received. Often our dreams are much bigger than just us. We have to believe we are worthy to receive such dreams, grow in understanding and also in the confidence of how to act upon them.

There are two types of dreams that are deeply personal to me — those that show me aspects of my destiny and calling; and those where He shows me, like on a map, my spiritual journey. In this particular dream, He reveals the importance of paths I have taken in the past and hints at the direction I am to follow in the future; He has taken me to this same 'dream place' several times over the last few years, each time showing me a bit more about where I currently am on the journey, or explaining more about where I have come from. How confirming and encouraging these dreams can be!

The interpretation of dreams is important, and like the dream itself, must be led and directed by Holy Spirit. It is true dreams can come from other sources; I have found that dreams that originate from the enemy generally leave me feeling totally confused and waking with great fear. Mind you, I have had quite a few 'scary' dreams — nuclear explosions, bombings, and the like — but they can be experienced without concomitant fear if they are from the Lord, for 'God has not given us a spirit of fear . . .' (2 Tim 1:7). When I have a dream I feel originates from the enemy, I simply come before the Lord, asking Him to show me where I may have allowed room for the enemy to work in my life, and then I come before the Lord in repentance. The Holy Spirit is so pleased to show us the error of our ways as we humbly seek Him! There is never any need for condemnation—He convicts us so we may grow in Him. There is no point staying in error when we don't need to!

I have found that stewarding my dreams by writing them down straight away has been very important. Even if I do remember the dream later on, it is so easy to forget details that may turn out to be quite important. If it is the middle of the night and I don't want to turn on the light, I make a note on my phone as a calendar entry so it's dated, or I use a headlamp and write in my journal. Yes, it is always easy to stay half asleep, but the discipline of waking up properly and writing it down allows us to steward our dreams. I have found out the hard way the discipline is worth it! For a brief while I stopped writing them down . . . and the dreams stopped! The link was obvious, and my repentance needed to follow.

Some questions I have found good to ask myself after having a dream are: *Who was in it? Where did it take place? What time period or season was the dream in? How did it make you feel? What unusual details did you notice?* Remember, God *wants* us to hear Him, so He will make it clear! Sometimes He even walks me through the dream several times until I get the point He wanted to make, and so I remember it. Oh, He is so good!

Now, I am able to understand many of my dreams almost straight away. Others require some research, and yet others require much prayer, meditation, and contemplation over many days, waiting upon the Lord for His prompts, His timing, but refusing to let go until the meaning is clear. It reminds me of Gideon; he kept going back to the Lord, asking Him questions. He didn't just receive orders and then set off with his own ideas.

Hearing from God and understanding His message is communication with a close friend. Think of it like a child's therapy session—we need to keep throwing the talking-ball back and forth, but the effort is always worth it. Usually I find that more significant dreams require more effort to understand; they hold great treasures, give me direction and enable me to step into the next stage of what the Lord is calling me to. Waiting on the Lord involves seeking and asking, but it also involves waiting for His perfect timing. He knows how long it will take you to figure out a dream and then act on it, and He orders time to account for that.

God gives us dreams. Our response is to value those dreams, discern their meaning in our lives, and then wait on Him!

11

Worship Wider

---

*Be in awe before his majesty. Be in awe
before such power and might! Come worship
wonderful Yahweh, arrayed in all his splendor,
bowing in worship as he appears in the beauty
of holiness. Give him the honor due his name.
Worship him wearing the glory-garments of
your holy, priestly calling!*
Psalm 29:2 TPT

Around the time I started to dream, we purchased a newer car—one with a good sound system! Now the worship music that had stood me in good stead at home could come with me in the car! I had such a limited range of music, and so my son and I headed to our local Christian bookshop where there was a plethora of worship music to choose from.

I started by selecting albums or artists with songs we knew from church. Then I went to the Bargain Bin, and not being highly technical, I simply chose albums with pretty covers or nice names! I found a few duds, and some didn't suit us, but mostly I was very pleased. So, off we went, bopping down the highway, playing—and at times blasting—worship music! It was pretty awesome, really! Such great music and good lyrics! So uplifting! My son discovered his favourite artist—Lauren Daigle. I found several I enjoyed too—United Pursuit, Casting Crowns, Jesus Culture, Elevation Worship. There is so much awesome music available these days! I felt like I had been under a rock, not knowing so much uplifting music was around!

Invariably I would move between laughing, singing, proclaiming and crying as I listened to the music as I drove; it moved my heart so much. When I was at home, I took to dancing around to music in my kitchen. What good exercise! But gradually, even that didn't seem enough. I loved worshipping His Name, but I just wanted to lift Him higher, higher! And so, I found myself asking, 'How do I worship you *more*, Lord? It just doesn't seem like enough. You are so worthy! What I else can I do to worship You and give You the honour You deserve?' I felt so restricted in my physical self, so unable to adequately offer Him the worship He deserved. So limited.

Paul is very clear when he writes to the Romans about what their *intelligent* and *logical* act of worship is (and isn't our society also one based on logic and intellect?!). 'Therefore, I urge you, brothers and sisters, by the mercies of God, to present your bodies [dedicating all of yourselves, set apart] as a living sacrifice, holy and well-pleasing to God, *which is* your rational (logical, intelligent) act of worship' (Rom 12:1 AMP). So, it is not even an extravagant act of worship to do this, but just a logical conclusion!

This is why, at regular intervals, sometimes with my body laid out on the floor, I find myself calling out to the Father, 'Show me Lord, what more can I lay down? What must I give you in order to honour and serve you better? Where do I not walk in alignment with You? Please, show me!' It is a deep cry of my heart—to honour Him and to walk closer to Him. And yet, parts of me keep trying to skimp out of the promise! It's like parts of my soul catch me by surprise, as if to say, 'Oh, I wasn't around that day, I'd never say that! Oh, don't catch me!'

Somewhere along this journey I told Him I wanted to give *everything* to Him. To give Him my *whole* life, not just some of it. And in so doing, my understanding of my call to worship is growing wider. A life surrendered and set apart to Him.

12

Just One Word

---

*There is a season (a time appointed) for
everything and a time for every delight and
event or purpose under heaven.*
Ecclesiastes 3:1 AMP

Several years ago, I watched a video encouraging people to choose a word to define their year ahead. Just one word. The idea was to help set a defining direction for the new year. Being a large-scale thinker, this really struck a chord with me, and for a few years, I practised the habit. As I started this journey towards God, there were years where I aimed for 'less'—less busyness, hopefully less stuff, less ... anxiety?! Yes, I think there was less anxiety! And then a new year dawned, and it seemed like it was time for *more!* Having removed so much from my life that had clouded my view of God, I was ready for more—specifically, more of God. More of His Word. More of Him.

Now, here I was, at the start of the next year already. I was really enjoying having more of God in my life. I was on to a good thing!

This felt so right. It uplifted me, it encouraged me. It helped me face life so much better. Having finally prised open a wee corner of this box of treasure called 'God,' I couldn't stop.

As I thought about what I wanted the new year to hold, one word summed up my desire: *Relentless*. I shared about *Relentless* with my husband as we sat in a café during the new year period and I remember his response being, *'Uh oh!'* Clearly, he knows me! I'm an all-or-nothing person. I just wanted to relentlessly pursue God and all He had for me. Finally, it seemed, in my early fifties, I was figuring out what this life was about; I still wanted *more*, and I was willing to pursue it, *relentlessly*.

But I realised I wasn't going to get there right away. Something needed to fall—in fact, looking back, there were a lot of things! Maybe it's a good thing I didn't realise at the time just what lay ahead. God seems to reveal to us just what we need for the moment; He knows how much we can handle. He knows us so well, why should this surprise me?

As I considered where I wanted to go, I realised the 'things' I needed to let go of were mindsets—assumptions in my faith, ideas about God and how He worked, beliefs about who I was . . . and so much more. So much had to fall away. Obviously, there were plenty of mindsets that were not really doing me much good!

There were so many 'boxes' my life and brain operated from. These regulated how I thought, what I read, how I perceived things, even my opinions of things. I began to realise my default ways of thinking didn't necessarily align with the heart of God, and this was limiting His work in my life. I knew they would have to go, but how should I start the process? I wasn't really sure . . . and so I bumbled along, seeking Him in His word for insight. Around the same time, I found some groups on Facebook that were focussed on spiritual growth. I vividly remember one fellow commenting he had done many food fasts and really, it wasn't all that difficult; what he did find hard was to fast from his attitudes and opinions. Wow! Those words spoke strongly to me as I considered my own mindsets.

And so began something which, more or less, continues today. When I observe something, I try to pause and consider, *'What do you say about this situation, God?'* When I react strongly in a certain situation, I try to stop, either in the moment, or later, to ask, *'Why did I react like that, Holy Spirit? What was at the root of my reaction? Where did that come from? Was my reaction coming from a place of pain? If so, what is the source of the pain? What do I need to bring before You, Lord, so You may heal me? In what way was my reaction not aligned with Your heart?'*

I've found the Holy Spirit is so happy to show us what lies in our minds and hearts when we come to Him in humble submission. He is oh so happy to walk us into the healing Jesus has already paid for us on the cross, as we come in humility, repentance and surrender!

13

Fear

The Lord is my light and my salvation—whom shall I fear? The Lord is the strength of my life—of whom shall I be afraid?
Psalm 27:1 NIV

Recently I journaled a prayer that almost seems ludicrous. Even I have to wonder at what I wrote!

My desire, Lord, is to walk through fearful places—places made, or meant, to bring me fear—so I may truly know You better, so I may more fully know You as my protector, my Lord, my canopy. Teach me to lay all my fear at Your feet and take up You instead. Thank you, Jesus, you want to walk with me through these dark places so I may learn to see Your light, even there.

I know God loves to answer these sorts of prayers. But I certainly haven't always been willing, or wanting, to lay down my fear!

It was the first Sunday of the New Year and I was filled with excitement! As the congregation stood to sing our last song, I felt a strong urge to move up to the first row to support a friend who I knew was struggling greatly. Oh, how I resisted! As a youth, the Holy Spirit had prompted me to go forward for an altar call, but the fact that everyone would see me had held me back, paralysed in fear. Fear seemed to be wrapped up with shame and rejection, and it had often kept me from stepping out. But now I was adjusting to a new paradigm. I was determined to respond to the promptings of the Spirit. To do as He led. And He said I was to go up and stand beside her!

Slowly, feeling so many eyes on me, I stepped out of my seat and walked forward to stand next to my friend. Except I *didn't* just stand there. When I got to the front, it seemed like she was not aware of my presence. I didn't want to scare her (at least, that was the rationale at went through my mind) and since she was sitting down, I sat down too. As I did, however, it was like the darkness and despair in my friend came over me too. I could feel it. Gently, I put my hand on her arm, to let her know I was there.

What happened next was the last thing I ever expected! In a flash, my friend leapt up, yelled at me to *never touch her again*, and ran out of the service. Did I say we were in the front row?! Did I say the church was full?! Did I mention there were visitors? At least people were singing loudly! The service finished and I sat there in shock. No one came over to me. I eventually got up and went out to morning tea, pretending nothing had happened, but inside I was a mess.

Part way through morning tea, someone said my friend had asked for me, and would I go to see her? I did, and we both apologised. We knew we hadn't meant to hurt each other. There were tears on both sides as we talked it through; even so, as I walked away I had so many mixed-up feelings going on: guilt, embarrassment, shame—*oh, the shame!*—and rejection. I felt like I had ruined a good sermon. Ruined the church. Ruined it for the new family who would surely not come back. It felt like I had ruined everything.

I cried for days, it seemed. Oh, how it hurt. Here I was, finally getting bold enough to step out of my fear, only to be firmly stomped on! The fact that I had also disobeyed what the Holy Spirit had *actually* asked me to do didn't help. Why had I sat when I had only been asked to *stand* beside my friend?

Thankfully, I had a few good friends I could confide in. Oh, how I leaned on them! Oh, how they carried me. And oh, how I cried out to God. What had I done? Why did I feel so *bad*? I had so very many questions. And then, somewhere in that mess of days, He spoke to me. At first, it was just an impression deep in my heart—soft, gentle words of love. The first two things, the strongholds, that needed to fall, He told me, were 'Fear' and 'Rejection.'

Why do we have to start with such big issues?! I cried out in pain at all the fear, rejection, and hurt I carried, and as I did, He somehow came, comforted me, and helped me get through. I was inspired to pray for my friend like never before, to cry out for her to be released from the place of darkness and despair she 'resided' in.

Going back to church the next week was extremely hard. Yet somehow, I did, and no one seemed to bat an eyelid, though I was *so* sure everyone was thinking about the incident from the previous week! All my times as an embarrassed schoolgirl told me so. But this was the year of seeking the Lord relentlessly, and though we were still only two weeks in, I could feel the presence of the Lord so clearly as I stood there the following Sunday and sang. Oh, how He reassured me and encouraged me! I could feel His power surging through my body like strong, hot, electricity. I was so sure everyone else could feel it too! It seemed so evident, no?!

Over the next two or three weeks, the pain of the moment gradually dissipated. The people around me treated me as if it had never happened. No one said anything. Was this grace? Forgiveness? I wasn't sure. Though I did know I had faced my fear and rejection. Still, they were such hard issues to let go of! Who would have thought they would be the first things to fall? 'Couldn't you start with something smaller and easier?' I asked the Lord. Obviously not!

Then He showed me the next issues I would have to confront—'order' and 'balance.' At least I had warning this time, because those seemed pretty big too! I could see it was necessary to address these things and to see them fall, but it was beginning to sound like this year would bring quite a bit of work—hard work!

Already, though, I had begun to feel so incredibly good—deep, deep inside. It was like something in me had been released, a craving for more. I realised as I went along, I was actually craving the healing touch of God in my life. Oh, how long I had waited for this! Even in my pain, the hunger for more of God and more of His healing was burning inside of me. I knew I needed more of Him, and I knew I would be willing to walk wherever He called me in order to have it.

14

Mindsets

---

*'No weapon forged against you will prevail, and
you will refute every tongue that accuses you. This
is the heritage of the servants of the Lord, and this
is their vindication from me,' declares the Lord.*
Isaiah 54:17 NIV

Not long after the incident in church, I visited our local Christian bookstore. Before Christmas, a particular book had 'leapt' off the shelf at me, but since I already had enough books to buy that day, I had decided to leave it till next time. Now, as I stood in front of the section once again, the same book seemed to really stand out to me. It was called 'Operating in the Courts of Heaven,' by Robert Henderson, and though it seemed unlike anything I had heard of or read before, I was intrigued nonetheless, and decided to purchase it. The book turned out to be incredibly eye opening—and incredibly challenging!

When I was younger, I had been at the receiving end of other people's mindsets and paradigms. Have you too? It's no fun! I encountered rejection because of who it appeared I was, or who I 'should' be, or conclusions people made about me from my clothes, my body shape, my skin colour, even my accent! This was all based on the perceptions people held, whether or not they were true. Usually they were not. But other people's opinions often hurt because they hit at our insecurities, our sense of value. We recoil at the thought of rejection.

Because of this, I didn't want to carry prejudices or untrue mindsets, though I knew I did. I didn't like them in my faith either. I just had this uncomfortable feeling there must be many different ways to worship and honour the Lord, therefore maybe I should not be quite so quick to judge others simply because their approach wasn't like mine. I even had a growing suspicion that my doctrine wasn't perfect either! I knew I was still missing something, and, knowing that the only one with perfect doctrine is God Himself, I began to suspect there were many things I needed to be willing to question—assumptions and attitudes I had to accept may be wrong. I had to be willing to accept that 'my' way of doing church or of 'doing God' might still be lacking. Maybe 'more' actually meant 'less' of my ideas! Having trained as a scientist, this made sense, but it significantly challenged me.

Reading about the 'Courts of Heaven' got me looking at Scripture in a new way, and yet... it all made sense! I was aware it was a fairly new topic in our generation, and definitely not 'mainstream,' and I was aware it was probably best not to open up to too many people about this! So I kept quiet and read the book bit by bit, then let it sit in my mind as I processed it, mulled over it and considered it personally. The concept of the 'Courts of Heaven' being a legal environment we could engage with, seemed quite 'out there,' and I didn't want to end up down some rabbit hole that was not of the Lord.

Still, I couldn't stop this nagging feeling the Scripture was clear and the Bible is indeed full of legal terminology. It was there for the seeing. And, the results of people who approached prayer within this legal framework were astounding. Praying 'in the Courts of Heaven' had obviously made a significant difference in many people's lives. These people were giving praise and glory to God. They were walking closer with the Lord. Entering the Courts of Heaven seemed to have enabled people to overcome many things, including mental illness, long-standing health issues and poor life choices. Now, they were walking into more of what God had for them; they were achieving their calling. Their use of Scripture seemed robust; and the fruit was solid.

Researching the topic, I found this revelation had come to quite a few people, of different backgrounds, usually quite separately. While people applied their understanding of the Courts of Heaven in slightly different ways, it all yielded solid results. For the time being, however, I kept the 'Courts of Heaven' concept in the back of my mind and continued my personal Bible study and time in the Word with the Lord, certain He would prompt me if I should take this information any further.

A few months later I had the opportunity to go away on my own for a few days to a silent retreat centre. What a treat! As I headed off with my stash of worship music for the car trip, I tried to ignore the familiar mild, numbing pain in my head. Migraine or not, I was going! As I pulled into the retreat centre, however, a strong stab of pain accosted me. The migraine was settling in, like it or not. But I figured I didn't have to drive anywhere for a few days, and so I settled into my room. I was determined a migraine was not going to get in the way of God speaking to me while I was there. So, as I lay down that night, I prayed He would use the time—and the migraine—in whatever way He wanted to.

During the night, the pain got stronger, and then, at some stage during the night I became aware I was in a vision. I had been paying attention to my dreams for a few months by now, but this was the first vision I was conscious I had experienced. I was awake, and yet I was aware I was being brought in to a room with the Holy Spirit escorting me on my left side and Jesus standing just off to my right. In the front of the room was a throne, or bench. I heard a voice from the bench, and there was also a voice off to the left of the bench, but I could not see anyone. Then something was placed across my shoulders—I could actually feel the weight of it physically. I seemed to know it was a mantle, though I didn't really know what that meant.

Suddenly, the pain rose in my head, and as it rose, a string of memories came flooding to my mind—old memories which were linked with great emotional pain. As each memory came to mind, my physical pain rose along with it, and I felt compelled to repent for the lies I had believed about all that had taken place. Out loud, I began asking the blood of Jesus to speak for me. As I looked across to Jesus, He nodded. I was also aware that my repentance and His 'nod' of approval was accepted by the 'bench,' at which point the severe pain in my head subsided, my body relaxed, and I could rest.

The first time I addressed an old memory it seemed odd, but after a while another physical pain rose in my head, and this time I cried out 'What is it Lord?' Then another memory would arise in my mind; sometimes it was a situation where I had not walked in a godly manner. With that, I would come before the bench, repent, and plead the blood of Jesus. Every time, the blood was accepted, and the pain would subside! This happened probably at least six times over the course of the night until, at last, the early light of sunrise was entering my room and I finally fell asleep with no more pain in my head!

I could no longer believe the Courts of Heaven did not exist. After returning from my retreat, I found a group that offered free prayer ministry in the 'Courts of Heaven.' I felt there were still issues to address, so after watching their procedure for a while I organised to receive prayer ministry. After addressing some generational issues, a small team of people who were Seers prayed over me and received either words or images regarding charges the Accuser was using against me, in order to attack me. There was a quite a list of words, but these were grouped, and in praying through the groupings of words privately over the coming week, I received clarity as to what each charge referred to. I was thankful for the ministry team who at times helped me understand the symbolic nature of the words given, and I was also amazed at how the Holy Spirit gave me understanding and revelation. As I came to understand the charges against me, I would come to the Lord in repentance to clear these charges in the Court. I was amazed at the freedom I experienced after these sessions!

One thing I noticed during this time was that I was quickly gaining a much deeper understanding of sin in my life! I was being taught to see sin as Father God saw it . . . and also as the Accuser saw it. Satan is a legalist, so you can be sure he picks up on every sin and uses them against us!

Suddenly I became much more aware of my actions, thoughts, attitudes and opinions. If they did not align with God's heart and His commands, and exalt the Lord, well then, it was sin. Simple! The stakes were raised. I stayed in this place of deep awareness and repentance for several months, and then, gradually I felt the Lord calling me on; not to leave this teaching altogether, but rather to add it to my 'arsenal' of prayer and warfare strategies, and move into the next stage of my healing and walk with Him.

15

Vision

---

*Open up, ancient gates! Open up, ancient
doors, and let the King of Glory come in!
Who is this King of Glory? The Lord strong
and mighty, the Lord mighty in battle.*
Psalm 24: 7-8 NIV

The healing I had received so far was significant and deep—it touched on my identity and self-worth. It also addressed aspects of my behaviour, and even things in my physical environment, that were enabling the enemy to gain access into my life. At the same time, I was growing in my understanding of the incredible power of the blood. Wow, the blood of Jesus is oh, so powerful!

One day, I was taking my son to his gardening job. As I drove, a friend who was having a hard time at work was on my mind. Her job carried much responsibility and her work environment was particularly difficult. Another friend and I had been praying for her, and I was thankful there were two of us because she was more 'regular' in her prayer-habit than me. For a while

I had gotten inconsistent in my prayers and even started believing that they didn't make a difference anyway. That always leads to a steep slippery slope! Lately, however, we had been more regular in our prayer and communication for our friend, and just as well, because her work situation was coming to a head.

So, there I was, just driving along the road, listening to worship music, thinking about the Lord, His love, His care, and how wonderful it was to pray and share with these two lovely women after God's heart. And then, as I looked at the road ahead, I saw, right ahead of me, a vision of a few people dancing. Then my view widened, and I could see a whole gathering of people playing their tambourines and dancing! Oh, what joy they exhibited as they freely danced and rejoiced. In my vision, they were making their way up an old cobblestone road, heading slightly uphill. Behind them were more dancers, all so exuberant as they rejoiced! It reminded me of David dancing as he came into Jerusalem—only here were many 'Davids'!

Behind the musicians and dancers, a beautiful, high carriage was being carried by many priests—His people! It had a large golden box in the middle—like the ark of the covenant. Above the box sat Jesus. He was on a throne or seat. Ahh, the mercy seat! The marriage carriage! Jesus was smiling broadly at all his worshippers—but in His spirit I saw that He was dancing too! And there were so many worshippers! Along the sides of the carriage, the roadway was lined with people all dancing in unison, waving flags and banners, and crying out with sheer *joy* as the carriage moved along. At the front of the carriage were intercessors, proclaiming the coming of the Lord as they danced. The whole scene was electric with energy and rejoicing! It was such a beautiful vision, and to this day, I can see it still!

I overflowed with joy, peace and delight as I wrote to my friends later that day to encourage them. 'Keep praising our awesome God!' I said. 'Rejoice over everything with praise. Lift His name high in every situation that the King of Glory may come in! Stay firm in the Lord, rejoicing over all He puts into our hands.'

Vision. It's such a hard thing to describe. And of course, I had no church background of it, nothing to guide me, although believing I could experience a vision was a positive place to start! I could tell the vision I had received was from the Lord; it glorified God, it exalted His plans, not mine, it aligned with Scripture, and I had a sense of peace both while seeing it, and afterwards.

I had no guidelines about how to develop in this gift of 'seeing,' yet I felt the Lord instructing me not to seek out information about it, but simply to seek Him. He knows me so well! He knows I can get carried away with things, that I possibly would have got stuck in seeking the gift, not the Giver. Even so, I have picked up some guidelines and tips along the way through snippets of teachings, looking at Scripture, and hearing other people talk about their visions and how they move through them. And each snippet is a special little treasure that has been revealed to me in God's timing.

Being able to see with spiritual vision has really made my prayer-life come alive! And maybe it's not so unusual. I'm sure many people have visions during prayer without realising it, pictures that flood their imagination while they are praying or ideas about what to pray for, or how to pray? Insights and revelation—these are all ways the Holy Spirit speaks to us. Sometimes He uses words, and sometimes He uses pictures. How wonderful it is when we can honour and acknowledge the Holy Spirit's leading as we pray. What if we were not afraid to wait? What if we simply waited for Him to take the lead? Oh, the joy I've found in sitting with the Lord to perceive what is on His heart before turning it into prayer.

16

One Cedar

But the godly will flourish like palm trees
and grow strong like the cedars of Lebanon.
Psalm 92:12 NLT

I was maturing in my prayer life and prayer language as I learned to honour and value Holy Spirit's ministry. I longed to lift up the Name of the One and Only and give Him all the glory He is due. Sometimes, however, the spiritual walk feels like a spiral. You face an issue, then you face it again, maybe from a different angle, or from an ever-deeper level.

Facing fear at the start of the year had been so hard that I thought, surely I had conquered fear once and for all! What I didn't know, was that when it came to conquering fear, I had only just *begun*! Now I began to see other places in my life where fear had gotten hold, and essentially still ruled. Once in a while, when it bubbled up to the top of my life, the Lord would gently make me aware of another area where I carried fear, and where He instead desired that I would know the wholeness of His love.

Like a sliver of wood stuck in a finger, often the process of festering would start slowly. Gradually, I would become aware that my intimacy with the Lord was, well, lacking something. It was like I was moving away from a deep awareness of His presence in my spirit. I still knew it all in my head. I still had close and precious times with the Lord, but as an issue began to rise to the surface there just seemed to be a distance growing between us. Instead of another layer of the onion being peeled off, it now felt like the onion layer was between the Lord and I! I wouldn't hear as clearly or easily.

And it's still often like that. Sometimes I feel more proactive and just say, *'Okay, Lord, tell me, what this it? I don't like this, let's get it over and done with!'* And then other times I get caught up with day-to-day 'doings' and I coast along, assuring myself I'm just busy and it will all be better once I just sit down with the Lord, once I get a more relaxed pace of life, and all the while the sliver moves a bit closer to the top. It gets more niggly. The skin gets a bit redder! I feel a bit less connected to the Lord. My worship doesn't seem as sincere, though my actions are as sincere as ever. There is just a growing restlessness within me. I love the peace and rest of communion with the Lord so much now, that when the shalom is disrupted, it grates on me.

This time, when the 'sliver' came to the surface, I realised it was fear again rearing its ugly head; another aspect of fear had emerged, and it was causing me to be agitated in my responses to those around me. This time, I really wanted to get to the bottom of the fear. To be rid of it once and for all. I could see by now that fear had become a 'stronghold' in my life—not just a passing issue to deal with. The impact of fear in my life may have been smaller than before, but still, I was sick of it. I had tried praying through it on my own, but it didn't seem to be budging; the fear kept coming back, I could tell it hadn't been property dealt with.

Then I remembered that in her book, *Feels Like I'm Breathing*, Anya McKee had described how she addressed strongholds in her life. She used the analogy of stronghold being like a fortress with walls. A stronghold effectively gave the enemy a place to legally operate from, a place from which to trigger negative emotional responses and render me weak and powerless in some area of my life.

When I read her analogy of a fortified city, my mind went to all the cities the Israelites had fought to conquer after they entered the Promised Land. I had long had a fascination with the metaphor of the Exodus and the subsequent journey of the people of God. If I was addressing a stronghold, did that mean I was now coming into His promises for me? What an exciting thought! Maybe I had finally left the wilderness and was battling through the Promised Land. What an exciting prospect!

I knew from Anya's story that when strongholds were broken, the enemy would lose his foothold, and I could indeed be free, not only of fear, but of the ungodly responses fear and rejection often triggered in me.

And so, I decided to give Anya a call. Together, in the early hours one morning, Anya, in prayer, gently walked me through tearing down this stronghold. Together, we identified the stronghold of fear in my life and brought it into the light. Then we asked the Holy Spirit to show us where it had started and how it had become so strong. Right then, I realised it had all begun in a moment of time when I was a little child in Kindergarten and had seen someone else being rejected. Fear and rejection had formed a strong alliance in my life, which over the years, had left me hurting and weakened. That morning, however, as Anya prompted me and I prayed through the moments in my life as the Holy Spirit highlighted them to me, I felt a growing sense of peace and calm.

As we continued to pray, replacing the lies of the enemy with truth from God's word and pouring forgiveness over each situation, I saw a beautiful picture of rough, fresh soil that had been freshly tilled. It seemed like the surroundings were a forest, except I couldn't see any trees—I just perceived that it had the soft shade of a forest. As I watched, a tree started to grow up out of the tilled soil. It was a strong tree, though it was not yet at its full size. I had an awareness in my spirit that the tree was a Cedar of Lebanon, and the tree was called 'Faith.' I also had the impression there should be other trees in the 'forest' also, but I couldn't see them, no matter how hard I looked into the scene. Where were they? How could it be a forest with only one tree?

And then, at the base of the tree was the compost it had grown out of. The compost also had a name. It was called 'Fear.' Through God's perfect love, my fear had been broken down, just like the walls of that fortress, broken down so it was no more than compost! Demolished fear was now rich soil for my faith to grow in!

17
Worship Deeper

For you are my dove, hidden in the split-open rock. It was I who took you and hid you up high in the secret stairway of the sky. Let me see your radiant face and hear your sweet voice. How beautiful your eyes of worship and lovely your voice in prayer.
Song of Songs 2:14 TPT

By now, my worship went beyond just singing and responding to music. Music still paved the way for me to enter into worship with my Lord, but music in itself did not constitute the extent of my worship. More and more, worship involved laying things down; surrender was becoming my newest expression of worship. Sometimes it was activities or time I surrendered to the Lord. Other times it was my personal, automatic response to what I saw around me. And sometimes it was those strongholds I had kept hidden for so long. Always, it was the laying down of striving in my own efforts and instead seeking His will, His way, His timing in each thing I faced.

As an act of worship, I was choosing to take my focus off this world and turn my eyes, my soul, my attention, away from the physical or emotional circumstances I found myself in and on to the truth of who God is. To focus solely on the great 'I AM.'

After working long hours doing some external contract work, I was tired! Finally, I had a day off, and I was aching for time with the Lord before heading off to an appointment later in the day. I had slept in, then spent time in the Word and prayer; now it was almost time to get up but I really wanted to just lie there in bed a wee bit longer enjoying the presence of the Lord! *'I just want to spend just a little bit longer with You this morning, Lord,'* I prayed. *'It is so good to sit in this place of peace and rest.'*

As I procrastinated for just a few more minutes, my eyes closed and gradually I became aware that I seemed to be walking up a narrowing tunnel. It wasn't all dark, it was just . . . dim. At the end of the tunnel, I came to a plain brown door, which I felt I was to open. As I turned the knob and opened the door, there was Jesus, standing there in the brightness, to welcome me! He had a huge, loving smile on His face. The setting was bright, but my eyes instantly adjusted as if they had not been in the dimness at all. He held out His hand to me and with an inviting tone said, *'Come!'*

As I stepped across the threshold, the background which had initially been only bright light, opened up into a garden scene—a beautiful, lush, green garden. The lushness implied that it was a tropical garden, but the 'look' of the garden didn't seem all that important. The overwhelming impression was the *atmosphere* of the garden. As I held onto Jesus' hand and looked up into His face, His eyes just beamed out love all over me! It was the same for the garden—it beamed and effused *love* over the whole place. It was like the garden was sitting within a completely loving environment, sending out 'love waves' into the air. The whole place was already so full of love that it didn't *need* anymore; it was complete with love. Yet the environment could do nothing else but emit more love!

As I walked hand in hand with Jesus, I came to realise that I was a young girl, about eight years old. I was enjoying the garden with the freedom and openness of a young child who just accepts the surroundings for what it is. I felt so comfortable walking with Jesus, more like I was walking with a big brother than with someone in authority. I felt safe, secure, completely happy, and at ease. At first, we walked along a grassy area with plants along the side, but then we came to a circular, grassy clearing. Beyond was a babbling brook of crystal-clear water, cheerfully leaping along. Next to the brook was a beautiful tree with bright, fresh fruit. I knew I could go and eat some fruit and that it would be good, but the stream beckoned me. I asked if I could go for a swim. Jesus, with a gleam in His eye, nodded His head, and immediately I was dressed in a burgundy bathing suit.

Without hesitation, I hopped into the water and played under the little waves, facing upstream and diving over and over again into the fresh, velvet-like water. It was such a fun time! After a while I felt like it was time to hop out, like there were other things to do now. I got out and instantly found myself in a young girl's dress that was right there, waiting for me. I could have had some fruit, but thought, *'I'll come back later and get that.'*

Jesus had waited patiently for me as I had enjoyed my swim, but now He asked me if I would like to go and see Father. *'Oh yes!'* I replied. I just never knew what to expect in this place! So much excitement rose up within me as He led me over to the edge of the clearing and there was my Heavenly Father, sitting on a rock. In a way, the setting was like a drawing from a Children's Bible. The same love that Jesus had pouring out of His eyes was also in the Father's eyes; it was like their eyes were connected.

I looked up to Jesus as if to check that I could go to my Father, and with a smile and a nod of His head I let go of Jesus' hand and approached the Father. He welcomed me with open arms, and I happily went right up to Him for a huge fatherly hug. It was as if I had always known how good that would feel. As if I already *knew* the feeling of His hugging arms around me, but just hadn't been there for a long time. Nothing else mattered but the big, surrounding 'bear hug' of my Heavenly Father. Hopping up onto His knee, I leaned against His chest, simply enjoying being with Him. He asked me if I'd like to hear a story. *'Oh yes!'* I responded. 'What would you like to hear a story about?' He asked, and instantly the thing that came to my mind (in the vision) was Enoch. He was my favourite Bible character, and yet there is so little written about him in the Bible.

As I sat there in anticipation it was like the story was suddenly but gently 'dropped' into my heart. I knew I had received the story, the 'knowing,' and yet not a single word had been spoken between us. Both Father and I knew the story, yet there were no words that could limit it. In that way the story could not be corrupted by my memory, nor could it be limited. It just *was*. We both sat there quietly enjoying the story as it sank in; we both knew the content, and though no word had been spoken, it made a beautiful impression on my spirit. Then after a bit, Jesus gently held out His hand and said it was time to go. I gave Father a hug, and as I hopped off His knee, I waved goodbye and took Jesus' hand to go. I had no hesitation in leaving because I knew I could come back.

Jesus and I walked back through the garden towards the doorway, not speaking and yet in perfect communication and fellowship. There seemed to be so few words in this place, yet the silence was never awkward, never empty. There were so many times when words didn't *need* to be spoken. The silence was just . . . *love*! When I knew it was time to go, there was no hesitation in my spirit to immediately obey. I took one parting look around as we approached the doorway, and as Jesus and I hugged goodbye, He reminded me that I could always come back, that this Secret Place would always be available to me. As I closed the door behind me and entered the dim tunnel again, I gradually became aware again of the bed beneath me.

It felt like this experience of the heavenlies had lasted for hours, yet when I opened my eyes and looked at the clock, only ten minutes had passed. It was the perfect time for me to get up. Wide awake, thoroughly refreshed, and sublimely at peace, I got ready for my shower. This physical world took on such a different hue now that I was so much more aware of the spiritual realm. I almost had to pinch myself! I knew what I had experienced wasn't just my imagination; for starters it was far beyond what my mind could ever have come up on its own! I felt like I was floating, yet I was totally able to engage with the details of the day. I carried a quality of love I had never known before, and this enabled me to interact with others on a new level of love and serenity. Having experienced His love, undiluted, in the spiritual realm, I now knew there was nothing that was not worth surrendering to my Father. His love was worth it all, it conquers all. I longed to carry His love, to be filled with love until it spilled over to the world around me.

18

Order

*Hear, O Israel: The Lord our God,
the Lord is one.*
Deuteronomy 6:4 NIV

When the Lord showed me that after Fear and Rejection, the next areas in my life to address would be *Order* and *Balance*, I thought I knew what he was referring to. I was wrong. I wonder how often we get God wrong?! I bet it's a lot of the time, actually. He always does so much more than we can ever imagine. Oh, how our 'boxes' constrain God and His work in our lives! Take, for example, how our understanding of God can be severely hindered by our understanding of love and goodness. When we bring our worldly understanding of these and try to project them onto God, who is other-worldly, oh how much we miss!

I have never felt like I am a person who was either ordered or balanced, so to have both in my life seemed like a really big ask. I had presumed God would simply speak to me about cleaning my house and bringing it into more 'order' (which I'm sure my husband would appreciate!). I thought having 'balance' in my life would mean not taking things to extremes like I tend to do, that somehow, I had to change to be less of an 'all-or-nothing' person. I thought He was going to be asking me to change who I am!

But I still hadn't got it! I still didn't understand that God neither expected *me* to change myself, nor did *He* want to change who He created me to be! As I began thinking about what God might want to do in me, I had forgotten that God loves me just the way I am, that He made me just the way I am, for His plans and His purposes! Yes, he wanted to purify me for His purposes, but who said anything about totally eradicating my whole character?! He simply wanted to purify me, not from the outside—from striving or 'doing' in a physical sense—but rather from the inside, from my spirit, and then, through my spirit to my soul and body. That is true, spirit-led, change from inside out.

Any changes my Heavenly Father wanted to bring about in my life needed to come from, and be directed by, Him. But I had to be willing to walk into what He wanted to show me. It always starts with our willingness to surrender; to lay our lives down at His cross and say, *'Take it all Lord, it is Yours.'* God is no bully. He waits until we come and lay ourselves down.

Over many months, I began to see the 'order and balance' God wanted to restore to my life had to do with *Him*. It was about asking me to consider where was God in my life. How were things ordered in my world? *Who was at the top of the pecking order?* Obviously, my Lord was growing in importance, but was I willing to put Him before other things? Was I willing to put Him before television, or social media? Was I willing to seek His plans for my family, not my own? Was I willing to pick up my Bible before picking up my phone? Would I be willing to seek the Lord's counsel before that of my friends? And would I have these same priorities both in easy and difficult times?

In Deuteronomy 6:1 the Israelites were given clear 'demands, decrees and regulations' to obey as they entered the Promised Land. In order to live well as God's people under God's reign and rule in their new land, they were to do two things: fear the Lord, and obey his commands. Handy to be warned!

This is where God took me for a while in order to teach me to fear Him and obey His commands. I seemed to experience quite strong spiritual attacks, but I kept crying out to the Lord: *'What is going on? Please Lord help me understand why I am under such attack?'* The Lord showed me Exodus 20:20 where Moses said to the people, 'Do not be afraid. God has come to test you, so that the fear of God will be with you to keep you from sinning.' He revealed to me that I was experiencing these attacks so I would have a greater awareness of the fear of the Lord. Well, it certainly worked! It kept me humble and it certainly reduced my desire to walk outside His commands. I'm not perfect by any means, but I am certainly more aware of the extent of His grace when I do stuff up! And I am much speedier to repent!

While God was teaching me about order, I also felt a strong pull to study Psalm 119, though I didn't understand its significance at the time. God does so much work that we never realise until later! I was intrigued by the way Psalm 119 spoke of the different commands of the Lord and how they were to be kept. There certainly is a lot in there! Psalm 119 actually uses eight different words to describe the 'commands' the Lord had given. And in

Deuteronomy 6:1 God tells the people through Moses that in the land they were about to enter and occupy, they '*must* obey' the demands, decrees, regulations He had given them. *Must.* That sounds pretty important! But then He gave a beautiful promise: 'If you obey all His decrees and commands you will enjoy a long life' (Deut. 6:2b NLT).

Then Moses went on to say, 'Hear, O Israel: The Lord our God, the Lord is one' (Deut. 6:4). Ahh, so that is what the Lord was trying to tell me—not only is he 'one' but He also needs to be my 'one and only,' my top priority. My obedience to His word and His commands are there to ensure that the Lord is truly 'Numero Uno' in my life. This is the fruit I long to bear. That He should have first place in my life.

Number one priority: God.

19

Balance

---

*Love the Lord your God with all
your heart and with all your soul
and with all your strength.*
Deuteronomy 6:5 NIV

I have always been a person who likes to represent concepts visually. Although I suspect I am more of a visual thinker than my son, I decided one day to try to represent some theological concepts in images or mind maps for him. I was trying to explain to him how often, in the world, God is primarily seen as either loving *or* just. For many people, it is hard to reconcile the fact that God can be both all-loving *and* completely just; they seem to contradict one another. Christians and non-Christians alike tend to lean toward one aspect of God over another, even when both are equally true! God is completely loving and totally just *all the time*. He resides in the place where these two traits overlap, like two perfectly overlapping circles on a mind map.

I've found there are many other concepts that also seem to overlap in God's economy. Take freedom and surrender, for example. God has used this idea of overlap to help me find the balance I need to walk with Him in the promised land of my life. It is the balance that enables my intimacy with the Lord to grow unhindered.

How are we to love the Lord, our God? With three parts of our being: heart, soul and body (strength). Jesus said, 'Whatever comes out of the mouth comes from the heart, and this is what makes a man unclean *and* defiles him' (Matt. 15:18 AMP). I feel my 'heart' represents my attitudes and opinions. Therefore, to walk in intimacy with the Lord, my heart needs to be aligned with His. In every situation, I am to share His heart, to make it mine, rather than to indulge in my own opinions, which would leave me defiled.

To have the Lord truly reign in my life, not only my spirit, but also my soul, needed to be under His rule. Along the way, I had heard our 'soul' typically described as having three parts: the mind, emotions, and will. Each one of these areas must be submitted to Him, not just our minds!

It's true that studying God's Word in a language I fully understand is an awesome privilege. But what is the purpose of my study? Is it to know God more and have Him reveal Himself to me? Do I study the Word to hear His voice? Or is it more of an academic exercise? If I approach the Bible *just* as a logical, rational exercise, I will not grow in my relationship with the Lord. And if I were to use what I learn to control, compare or condemn others, then I have a very large plank in my own eye (Matt 7:1-5), and am clearly not focussed on God! My closeness with the Lord would certainly suffer if I chose this approach. It is not my role to condemn others in their walk, but to edify and encourage them. I can build up my mind with academic knowledge, or I can surrender it to the Lord and allow Him to transform me by renewing my mind (Rom 12:2). Then I will be able to walk more in line with the mind of Christ (1 Cor 2:16).

What is true of our minds is also true of our emotions. Our emotions are an important part of us and our faith, and not to be dismissed. However, they are not to be the driving force in our faith. We get to know God by experiencing Him, and just like in my relationship with my husband, I find my emotions are an important part of that. But if I based all my decisions within my marriage on how I was feeling at the time, I might have had a very short marriage! And if I were only willing to accept 'happy' experiences with my husband, I would miss out greatly on the blessing of marriage. To walk in my promised land, I must keep my eyes on my Lord through thick and thin, experiencing Him regardless of my emotions at the time. It will make our journey that much better to know Him in all the seasons of our lives. We may not always 'feel,' or be aware of, His presence, but we can still *know* in our heart He is with us. We can choose to worship and walk in His ways regardless of how we feel at any given time.

Likewise, I notice that my will plays a clear role in determining if I walk in ongoing intimacy with the Lord, although not my will *per se*, but what I do with my will. As I allow the Spirit of God to have control of me, He in turn produces 'self-control,' enabling me to submit to God's will and desire for my life in each and every circumstance. My surrender allows me to esteem Christ, and Him alone, over my mind, my emotions, or my own desires. God always gives me free will; it's one of the hallmarks of His love for us. It's then up to me to lay my free will down before Him. A submitted will enables me to seek the Lord's face when it doesn't feel good, to trust His Word, even when I don't understand it yet, to seek the Giver, not the gift. It frees me to appreciate my gifts and desire to grow in them, but at the same time continue to uphold God, the Giver of the gift, even higher, so that even if there were no gift, I would still proclaim His Name and love, honour and adore Him.

I have found the balance of intimacy is the 'middle' road, the narrow path, that leads deeper into His heart. At times, He allows me to walk a little off course so I may experience, and come to know, the difference. But it's always my choice to surrender to God. And it's also my choice to come before Him in humility and repentance when I walk off the narrow path of intimacy.

The restoration of order and balance brings me to a place of bliss and intimacy with my Lord. A place I cannot resist!

20

Forest of Cedars

But the godly will flourish like palm trees
and grow strong like the cedars of Lebanon.
For they are transplanted to the Lord's own
house. They flourish in the courts of our God.
Even in old age they will still produce fruit;
they will remain vital and green.
Psalm 92:12-15 NLT

The Courts of Heaven process had removed some major roadblocks in my spiritual life and helped my understanding of sin. I also felt I had mostly dealt with generational issues, at least for now. Praying with Anya had helped me demolish the stronghold of fear. But there were still many other areas of my life where I had experienced wounding, and those wounds led to poor responses in me. It still seemed there were many areas of woundedness in me, and I didn't even know what they all were! So I continued to search. Obviously, I needed more healing.

A common denominator emerged through all the prayer ministry I received; my areas of wounding all involved lies that I was believing! Now I felt I needed a more organised way of dealing with them, rather than just addressing them haphazardly as they rose their ugly head in my life. By this stage I was aware there were lots of lies that I had come to believe. Surely there was some sort of organisation to the ones that seemed to rise up?

Through a course at a nearby ministry centre, I became aware of the book, *Healing the Wounded Heart* by Thom Gardner. What struck me was how he related the types of wounds our hearts encounter, to the names of the seven main tribes that the Israelites fought in the Promised Land. My ears pricked up. There was that 'Promised Land' theme again! In his book, Gardener groups our wounds under the areas of fear, rejection, worthlessness, shame, insecurity, defilement, and hopelessness. That made sense to me — and I could easily see I carried wounds in each area! How wonderful to find a resource that could clearly provide a road map for healing! While I had (at least partially) addressed some of these areas already, others still needed much work. I stopped occasionally as I read the book to process each step along the way.

At one stage, I put the book down for several months and forgot about it. Then, that sliver in the finger thing started happening again! The Lord was bringing some issue to the surface in my life. I had days of feeling crabby, of praying but not knowing exactly what I was praying for, days of being aware of sin, but not knowing what sin to repent of! *'Lord, how can I repent if I don't know what it is? Open my eyes, Lord,'* I prayed. I was in a place of stagnation, trying for breakthrough, but it wasn't coming.

Then, after days of walking around the fortress walls of 'whatever-it-was', finally the scales on my eyes came down. It was *shame* I was dealing with. Of course! It was hard to see because a stronghold of shame tries to hide. But praise God, He led me back to Thom Gardner's book. Ironically, I had stopped reading it three pages before the chapter on shame! But hey, I wouldn't have recognised that I carried it at the time anyway. God's timing is perfect. It was so wonderful to finally read the chapter and walk through the process of prayer and forgiveness into the healing available through the blood of Jesus. Finally, I began to experience freedom and walk in the lightness that came from pouring forgiveness over me and the trials of my past in that area.

With the fall of each stronghold and the healing of each wound, it felt like I was finally walking into more of the spiritual health and freedom I was seeking. *Yay* for freedom — the freedom bought through the blood! Now I was experiencing freedom from captivity, freedom to walk more into the peace and wholeness that God intends for us to dwell in and for which Jesus has already paid the price. Finally, I was finding the freedom from which I could *abide* in my Lord, and *adore* my Lord. Yes, *that* is where I am meant to live! I am meant to live in my Promised Land *now*, so I may walk into my destiny *now*, and bring glory and honour to His name *now*!

Every once in a while, God would show me those cedars again. The first tree was getting larger, it was growing in circumference, as well as height. And other trees in the forest had grown up now too! Hope. Joy. Grace. Peace. Acceptance. Love. Each one of these trees had grown up out of the compost of specific lies that I had held on to, but now, as the pain, trauma and lies were composted, beautiful trees had emerged. Tender forest grass had sprung up, and I saw sweet little flowers dotted around—tender, pretty, white three-petaled flowers, reminiscent of the trillium that grows in the forests of southern Canada. God has grown a cedar forest in my spirit! The lies are breaking down and being composted, and from there is emerging my new life.

It was a most beautiful picture—and it got more beautiful each time I saw it. But there was one thing that bothered me. One tree on the left-hand side of the forest was much smaller than all the other ones; it was a sapling—skinny and short, still waiting to grow. The tree's name was 'Trust,' and it was the last tree to sprout up. It had always bothered me that it was so small. Yet, I couldn't seem to hasten its growth.

I had to accept I could not set the timing for that tree to grow. Only in the Lord's timing would it finally mature.

21

Little Foxes

You must catch the troubling foxes, those sly little foxes that hinder our relationship. For they raid our budding vineyard of love to ruin what I've planted within you. Will you catch them and remove them for me? We will do it together.
Song of Songs 2:15 TPT

Well, it's been quite the journey, and you may be pleased to know I'm not perfect yet!

I have appropriated the blood of Jesus over my life; I have painted it on the doorposts of my life. The sorrows that have wounded so many generations are healed and the strongholds I have identified are finally broken down. Praise God for the awesome powerful blood of Jesus that breaks strongholds and brings new life!

The journey is not over; there are still battles to face. But they seem smaller now, and more manageable. Instead of feeling like I'm up against a fortified town, now it's more like fighting skirmishes in wide open fields. The battles are smaller, less frequent and easier to discern. I am more experienced at appropriating the blood now. And *most* of the time I am less stubborn about surrendering the battle to the Lord! Much more of the time when the Lord shows me my old sin habits, I am willing to lay them down. Mostly! Of course, He is patient with me as I cry out to Him, '*Help me surrender this Lord. Help me even in my disbelief.*'

For me these are the issues the Bible describes as 'little foxes.' The little battles are no less important. They still impede my journey to Zion, so they must be addressed. In fact, I suspect that if they are not, they will grow, for where I am not willing to lay something down before the Lord, that weakness makes an opening for the enemy to get in. And he always utilises any opening into my life, which means if I am not willing to lay down one thing before the Lord, trouble will likely follow. Pride has a way of doing that! I suspect that is partly how those strongholds got so strong in the first place!

There are still many places where these new ways of living and responding to the world need to be walked out, areas that test whether the 'trees' in my life are strong and will continue to grow. They are ongoing. We always need to stay open to what the Lord is doing, and what He is calling us to.

Just a few months ago, I felt the Lord prompting me to fast. I wasn't yet aware of what the Lord was calling me to fast from— or for. I have found that, for me, a fast can either be for the purpose of removing something specific *from* my life for a while, or can be about adding something *in* (which of course necessitates removing something else). Just as I needed the Lord's leading to fast, I wanted His direction as to how I should fast and for what purpose. It was a busy time of year, but I kept declaring my willingness to fast and trusted that He would reveal it to me in His time.

Driving home one day, the Lord revealed to me what I was to do. I needed to climb a large hill near our home every day for the next twenty-one days and sound my recently-acquired shofar. I'll be honest, I was pretty out of shape—what He was asking of me would certainly be possible, but hard. Still, I figured that if He had asked me, then He knew I could do it, and I could do it with Him. So off I set the very next day.

It is difficult to explain how much good came out of that fast! The one or two hours a day of walking and talking with the Lord were so serene. And I did get fitter! But one day, probably into the third week, as I was wandering home, I realised I had been climbing a large hill—some might call it a mountain—every day!

With that realisation, I suddenly had a memory from about ten years earlier when I had been on a trip with my family. It was the first day of January, in Australia, and it was hot! We were visiting a National Park and despite the extreme forecast for the day, my husband and son and I decided to head out for a morning walk. I admit that right from the start I wasn't keen. The decision only came about because I was outnumbered! With every step it just seemed to get worse. My knees hurt, I was hot, I was sticky. Whenever I climbed, I was having trouble breathing in the thick, soupy air. I dragged myself along, making it quite clear to my family that I wasn't impressed, and it was their fault for ruining my new year on the very first day of it. In reality, I behaved more childlike than my son, who was about nine years old at the time. In fact, he was having fun!

But as I stumbled along the path, mumbling to myself, I realised, *'Wait, this is my life and I'm not having fun. I'm not enjoying this year. I do not have to do this!'* When I finally caught up to my family, as they waited patiently on the side of the track for me, I declared, 'That's it. I'm not doing hills anymore. You can take me for a walk, but I won't be under any obligation to walk up a hill again, especially just to appease someone else.'

Now, ten years later as I walked home, I realised I had spoken a word-curse over myself, and, now, by God's strength and power, I had just broken it! I had just *enjoyed* climbing a very large hill every day for three weeks! Hallelujah! But that was just one aspect of the good that God brought out of that fast. God always works on so many levels at once, so many that we often don't realise. We may not realise them till later, or maybe until we get to heaven. We so underestimate Him.

The Lord is indeed changing me! He is truly making me a new creation—breaking off the chains. Oh, so many chains—strongholds, curses I have spoken over myself, as well as the ones I have taken on from others. And it feels very . . . *good*! There is no stopping God. Not when He has a surrendered heart to work with. It's so nice now to be capturing these foxes together with Jesus!

22

Obedience

The Lord watches over those who obey Him,
those who trust in His constant love.
Psalm 33:18 AMP

The beginning of a new year was once again approaching and I was considering whether I should participate in a fast with some friends during the month of January. At the time, I 'just so happened' to have a conversation with a friend who told me about her walk with the Lord over many, many years. As she spoke about obedience, I realised that there was nothing 'just so happened' about what she said at all! In fact, God's hand was all over that conversation!

I was certainly more intentional about obeying the Lord and His ways now than I had ever been, but as she talked, it didn't take too much to get me thinking about the many ways in which I was still being disobedient—not 'specifically' to God, but in my life in general. As I stood at the kitchen bench preparing dinner one night shortly after our conversation, I said out loud to myself, 'Why, I can't even obey an alarm clock to get out of bed!' It was true! I am the sort of person who sets their alarm clock five or ten minutes early so I can lie there for a few minutes contemplating the day before I move; and really no alarm clock should be able to make *me* leap out of bed! I always admire my husband for that amazing ability—it certainly makes for a good employee.

But as soon as I spoke those words, it was like a sense of quiet encompassed me, so that in my spirit those words reverberated. And in that moment, I knew what my fast was to be—a sleep fast! For twenty-one days, I would set my alarm for three a.m., and I would get up when my alarm went off.

Every night, I set my alarm as a mark of willingness, but I found I only needed it the first night. In the end, the Lord woke me up when He wanted to! It was just my job to obey. I admit there were a few nights when I woke up at about midnight or one a.m. and thought, O*h, not yet, can I please just sleep a bit longer?* I'm sure I missed some treasures of revelation on those occasions, but I won't dwell on that. It was a learning process.

Initially, I had no idea what I was meant to do when I got up, so I'd just play a few beautiful worship songs. But after a few nights, as I got better at being awake at that time of night, I added in reading Scripture and sometimes journaling as well. Sometimes I would stay up for several hours. It was such a peaceful, quiet time.

Around half-way through the twenty-one days, I came back to a question I had often asked the Lord. I asked Him to explain to me more about the tabernacle in the desert. There is so much rich symbolism there. I knew I didn't yet understand enough about the tabernacle itself, or its meaning and that there was more to be unpacked, and in the last week, He started showing more to me. The glory and beauty of His revelation, as I sat and read my Bible and journaled in those quiet hours was priceless. The peace-filled friendship that it created made me crave those middle-of-the-night hours. I looked forward to them so much that at the end of the fast I asked, 'This time is awesome Lord, can I keep doing it?' But I felt I was to stop for the time being. Still, I had experienced the great beauty, intimacy and refreshing that was to be had in obedience.

Yes, obedience has blessings within it. You may think that getting up in the middle of the night is an odd way to learn it. Well, it's obviously one I needed to learn! And it wasn't the only area I needed to learn obedience. God has been finding more of those areas too! Many more.

For some reason, the larger, or more 'obvious' situations He calls me to walk in obedience to Him seem easier. I think that's because I perceive them to have more value. Or perhaps, in some instances, it is because I think someone else may notice. Which tells me there is still some of that 'fear of man greater than fear of God' issue hanging around! Do I only value obedience sometimes? I've realised I find obedience easier when I am specifically aiming be obedient. I am starting to more fully realise there is inconsistency in my walk with the Lord.

God is calling me to obedience in a range of areas. Some are incredibly small and I suspect that is because they are particularly weak! I can see I don't value obedience in the small things. But it is becoming evident that God *does* value obedience there! Like flossing my teeth every night, whether I think I need to or not. Whether or not I feel like it.

He is teaching me to be obedient to His Word which, of course, means reading and studying it with Holy Spirit and applying it in my life—being obedient to what I am learning. I have gotten better at that over the last few years. But now He is also calling me to obedience to His subtle promptings. He is calling me to immediate obedience, which means I need to constantly practise discerning His voice, His *rhema* word in my life. I always used to tell my son, 'Delayed obedience is disobedience.' Now it's my turn to truly learn that too!

Obedience. Immediately. Consistently. Even in the small things. These are the lessons He is walking me through now. I am encouraged when I remember the verse in Luke 16:10 where Jesus motivates us by saying, 'The one who manages the little he has been given with faithfulness and integrity will be promoted and trusted with greater responsibilities.' I am learning to be faithful, even in the little acts of obedience, even to the commitments I make with my own mouth.

Obedience is taking on a new meaning for me, a new fragrance. As I give Him my obedience, it becomes a way to worship and honour Him. And to worship Him always brings such deep joy, beyond imagining. What a joy to sacrifice to my Lord.

Over these past few months, as I have walked the path of learning more about obedience, I keep being reminded of the old hymn:

> *Trust and obey, for there's no other way,*
> *to be happy in Jesus, than to trust and obey.*

And so, as I submit myself in obedience to Him who is my *All in All*, I believe that last tree, the tree called 'Trust,' has been able to flourish. Praise be to God for His ongoing work.

23

Worship Higher

---

*But you have come to Mount Zion, to the city of
the living God, the heavenly Jerusalem.
Therefore, since we are receiving a kingdom that
cannot be shaken, let us be thankful, and so
worship God acceptably with
reverence and awe.*
Hebrews 12: 22,28 NIV

Since God first showed me those cedars growing in the forest of my spirit, I have learned that cedars of Lebanon are known for surviving challenging environments; they are said to be strong, to symbolise resilience, immortality, and elevation. And they were used in the building of Solomon's temple. Their roots are known to be as deep as the branches are high. Why, that sounds just like the sort of person I want to be! Oh, that the Lord's temple truly be built in my life, just as King David wrote in Psalm 92!

Oh, thank you Lord for calling me and pursuing me, so that I may come and walk closer with You. Thank you, Lord that through Your blood shed for me I receive healing and wholeness. You fight all my battles for me, and You give me the victory! Thank you for showing me how to truly worship You with all my life, not just with lifeless words. Please never stop showing me how I can worship You more. Please always show me when I go astray and give me the strength to walk back to You in repentance.

Lord, to lay my life before You in worship is such a joy. Indeed, You make my joy complete. Oh Lord, please continue to develop a tabernacle, like the one David resided in, within my heart that I may sing and play music before You, coming before you with my voice and instruments in prophetic worship; with new songs that come from Your heart entwined with mine. I come before You with thankfulness and praise, lifting up Your Name like David did on Mount Zion, with clapping, dancing and shouting, in reckless, exuberant celebration. There is indeed one thing I seek, and it is to dwell in Your presence all the days of my life, and to gaze upon Your beauty (Psalm 27:4).

Do whatever You need to do in my life so that I may minister before You in adoration and praise. Oh Lord, build my roots deep in You, so that I may soar with You and bring a sacrifice of praise before You. Oh Lord, grant that each day left of my life here I would walk closer with You so that, just like Enoch, when the day comes to go Home to You, it doesn't seem very far to walk at all.

Thank you, Lord that all along You knew my deepest heart's desire was to grow and be transplanted to Your house, to flourish in Your courts, and to produce fruit, lasting fruit, for You. I will declare Your praises for all of eternity! Thank you for leading me along the path and growing that beautiful forest within, Your very tabernacle. My good, good Father.

24

Adore. Abide.

It's who you are and the way you live that count before God. Your worship must engage your spirit in the pursuit of truth. That's the kind of people the Father is out looking for: those who are simply and honestly themselves before him in their worship. God is sheer being itself—Spirit. Those who worship him must do it out of their very being, their spirits, their true selves, in adoration.
John 4:23-24 MSG

At this stage of my journey, I have leaned two things.

Firstly, we were made to *adore God*. This is the chief aim of my life. It is the highest calling on my life. I was made to worship an awesome God. One who is outside space. Outside of time. Creator God. Jesus paid it all so I may worship my Heavenly Father in spirit and in truth.

So I may come before the throne of grace and mercy and bring Him adoration.

So I may lay down my life before Him as a fragrant offering.

And secondly, we were made to *abide* in God. I was made to live in constant, intimate, communion and fellowship with this awesome God! We *all* are. I was made to consistently dwell in His peace. Jesus paid it all for me, so I can be immersed, ensconced, in Him.

To be *one* with Him, starting now!

Adore. Abide. That is what we are made for.

I think I'm starting to understand it now, Lord!

Suggested Resources

BOOKS

Drawing Near
by John Bevere

Feels like I'm Breathing
by Anya McKee

Healing the Wounded Heart
by Thom Gardner

Operating in the Courts of Heaven
by Robert Henderson

MINISTRIES

Angel Ministries (Anne Graham Lotz)
www.annegrahamlotz.org

Aslan's Place (Generational and specific warfare prayers)
www.aslansplace.com

Communion with God Ministries (Two-way journaling)
www.cwgministries.org

'Don't Forbid Speaking in Tongues' by John Bevere
www.youtube.com/watch?v=eKB0wjVrvFM

Ellel Ministries (Inner healing and deliverance)
www.ellel.co.uk

Jubilee Resources (Generational Prayers, also for freemasonry)
www.jubileeresources.org

Messenger International (John and Lisa Bevere)
www.messengerinternational.org

Torn Curtain Collective (Jeff and Anya McKee)
www.torncurtainnz.com

Acknowledgements

Numero Uno. God, of course! Thank you, Lord, for leading me to write and encouraging me all the way along, for showing me what to write, and giving me the courage and the words to write the things I found hard. Thank you for helping me to understand my walk more as I have written this story.

My Family. Thank you so much to my husband and son especially, who have walked this journey with me, while most of the time they had no idea what was going on inside of me! Thank you for your incredible love for me, and patience with me! Thank you also to my wider family, for your great love.

Anya McKee. God is so good to give me such a wonderful friend like you and for bringing us back together again after so many years! Thank you for your extreme patience with me through this whole process. Thank you for encouraging me and giving me the confidence to step out.

My Prayer Call Family. Hanging out with all of you over the last eighteen months has been such an incredible joy in my life! Thank you for a safe place to grow in my walk and for the cover under which this book was written.

Spiritual growth can be messy! Thank you so much to so many of my friends who have walked this journey alongside me—for putting up with me in the messy times, praying with me, and for me, in the hard times, and encouraging me many times. I value your grace and forgiveness. I greatly appreciate your input into my life.

www.ingramcontent.com/pod-product-compliance
Lightning Source LLC
Chambersburg PA
CBHW050319010526
44107CB00055B/2315